ALTERNATIVE KILNS & FIRING TECHNIQUES

ALTERNATIVE KILNS & FIRING TECHNIQUES

Raku   Saggar   Pit   Barrel

James C. Watkins &
Paul Andrew Wandless

LARK BOOKS

A DIVISION OF STERLING PUBLISHING CO., INC.
NEW YORK / LONDON

Editor:

Suzanne J. E. Tourtillott

Art Directors:

828 Inc.

Kathy Holmes

Photographer:

Evan Bracken

Cover Designer:

Barbara Zaretsky

Illustrator:

Randy Brodnax

Assistant Editor:

Nathalie Mornu

Associate Art Director:

Shannon Yokeley

Editorial Assistance:

Delores Gosnell

Rebecca Lim

Special Photography:

David Jones and
   The Crowood Press 25, 128

Linda Keleigh 25

Suzanne Tourtillott 10, 11,
   89 (top right), 117 (left), 124

Anna Vogler 15

Notes About Suppliers:

Usually, the supplies you need for making the ceramics in Lark books can be found at your local ceramic supply store or retail business relevant to the topic of the book. Occasionally, however, you may need to buy materials or tools from specialty suppliers. In order to provide you with the most up-to-date information, we have created a listing of suppliers on our Web site, which we update on a regular basis. Visit us at www.larkbooks.com, click on "Craft Supply Sources," and then click on the relevant topic. You will find numerous companies listed with their web address and/or mailing address and phone number.

The Library of Congress has cataloged the hardcover edition as follows:

Watkins, James C., 1951-
  Alternative kilns & firing techniques : raku, saggar, pit, barrel / By
James C. Watkins & Paul Andrew Wandless.
     p. cm.
Includes index.
  ISBN 1-57990-455-6
  1. Kilns. 2. Firing (Ceramics) 3. Pottery craft. 4. Raku pottery.
I. Wandless, Paul Andrew. II. Title.
TT924.W38 2004
738.1'36--dc22   2003022198

10 9 8 7 6 5 4 3 2

Published by Lark Books,
a division of Sterling Publishing Co., Inc.
387 Park Avenue South, New York, N.Y. 10016

First Paperback Edition 2006
© 2004., James C. Watkins and Paul Andrew Wandless

Distributed in Canada by Sterling Publishing,
c/o Canadian Manda Group, 165 Dufferin Street
Toronto, Ontario, Canada M6K 3H6

Distributed in the United Kingdom by GMC Distribution Services,
Castle Place, 166 High Street, Lewes, East Sussex, England BN7 1XU

Distributed in Australia by Capricorn Link (Australia) Pty Ltd.,
P.O. Box 704, Windsor, NSW 2756 Australia

The written instructions, photographs, designs, patterns, and projects in this volume are intended for the personal use of the reader and may be reproduced for that purpose only. Any other use, especially commercial use, is forbidden under law without written permission of the copyright holder.

Every effort has been made to ensure that all the information in this book is accurate. However, due to differing conditions, tools, and individual skills, the publisher cannot be responsible for any injuries, losses, and other damages that may result from the use of the information in this book.

If you have questions or comments about this book, please contact:
Lark Books · 67 Broadway, Asheville, NC 28801 · (828) 253-0467

Manufactured in China

ISBN 13: 978-1-57990-455-5 (hardcover) 978-1-57990-952-9 (paperback)
ISBN 10: 1-57990-455-6 (hardcover) 1-57990-952-3 (paperback)

For information about custom editions, special sales, premium and corporate purchases, please contact Sterling Special Sales Department at 800-805-5489 or specialsales@sterlingpub.com.

CONTENTS

OUT OF THE KILN, INTO THE FIRE

Ceramists have a primal fascination with the power of fire on clay. It is for these artists and aspirants that we wrote this book on raku and other postfiring reduction methods. We believe that you'll find these fast-firing techniques attractive because they yield such rich texture and color. Clay artists are often intrigued by the fleeting marks that are made when clay, heat, and smoke interact. The serendipitous nature of these low-temperature firing processes makes discovery as significant as invention. There are so many variations in the techniques described and illustrated here that your results will be limited only by your imagination.

We invited ceramic artists Randy Brodnax, Don Ellis, and Linda Keleigh to help us demonstrate their firing methods for this book. The five of us came together with a commitment to share with you all of our secrets based on our years of experience. Randy and Don are showmen as well as accomplished artists. They have worked together for many years, giving workshops all over the United States and sharing the alchemy of their methods; the breadth of their knowledge is amazing. We asked Linda to demonstrate the barrel-firing technique she uses to achieve rich, overlapping textures based on her painstaking attention to surface detail.

After much planning and working in the studio, we met on the top of a mountain in western North Carolina. The picturesque nature of the mountainous view was stimulating and invigorating. We watched the morning clouds roll out as the sun burned away the moisture and illuminated our stunning vista of the Blue Ridge Mountains. Providence was with us—so many things might have gone wrong!—for the weather was agreeable, and each technique we demonstrated yielded spectacular results. To top it off, Randy is a Cajun cook, so we had a big "wrap" party to celebrate our successes and cement our friendship. It was an idyllic place to work together and to enjoy the inspiration of nature and fellow artists.

We have included straightforward information about how to perform Western-style raku, as well as pit and barrel firings. We demonstrate saggar, low-temperature salt, alcohol reduction, and precious-metal fuming techniques, with plenty of information on alternative firings and tips for these various processes.

James C. Watkins
Bottle Form, 2002
11 x 9 in; Duncan Antique Brass
glaze Δ 04; sprayed gold luster Δ 019;
stannous chloride–fumed at 800°
(427°C); fired to Δ 012 in metal
saggar with toilet paper reduction
Photo by Hershel Womack

Paul Andrew Wandless
Not Quite Well, 2003
12¹/₂ x 9 x 5¹/₂ in
(31.8 x 22.9 x 14 cm);
aluminum-foil saggar;
alcohol reduction
Photo by artist

James C. Watkins
Bird Basket, 2000
15 x 10 in (38.1 x 25.4 cm);
Duncan Antique Brass glaze;
masking-tape stencils; fired to Δ 04
and cooled to 800°F (427°C);
stannous chloride fuming
Photo by Hershel Womack

There's a detailed plan on how to build an affordable, versatile, and easily constructed raku kiln that can be used for the majority of the techniques you'll see demonstrated, plus instructions on how to convert a gas burner to propane. As a bonus, Randy builds his unique wood-fueled Downdraft Stovepipe Barrel Kiln.

We feel that the included techniques offer students at every stage of their development the full scope of the ceramic process—the science of firing and the effects of chemistry—in a relatively intimate and immediate setting. The steps throughout these learning processes occur rapidly and with hands-on involvement. What makes this book unique is it illustrates all the process from beginning to end, including the convincing results from each demonstration. If you are a beginner, this book will assist you in learning the basics; if you are a mature clay artist, we believe the book will supply you with information that will enhance your knowledge and satisfy your thirst for new and exciting techniques.

Artists submitted nearly 500 slides for the gallery in this book, of which only a relative few could be included. This represents only a fraction of the number of clay artists interested in fast-fired, low-fired, and postfired reduction processes. The gallery sections show the breadth of amazing work produced by artists who use these techniques and sometimes they share their firing "secrets." Looking at the work, it is evident that these artists enjoy researching their processes with vigor and, in some cases, great patience. It is our belief that working with rapid-firing techniques exemplifies a marriage between the artist and chance. As the scientist Louis Pasteur once noted, "In the fields of observation, chance favors only the mind that is prepared."

Our hope is that as you explore the processes demonstrated in this book you'll have as much fun as we had at the top of the mountain in western North Carolina.

James C. Watkins and Paul Andrew Wandless

Paul Andrew Wandless
Collected Thoughts, **2003**
18¹/₂ x 12¹/₄ x 4¹/₄ in
(47 x 31 x 10.8 cm); low-temperature glazes and aluminum-foil saggar; alcohol reduction
Photo by artist

Before you begin reading about how to get great textures and colors on postfired ceramics, it will be helpful for you to know how this book is organized. *Alternative Kilns & Firing Techniques* is divided into three main sections: raku, pit, and barrel. In each section, you'll learn first how to build simple, yet effective, types of kilns. But these kilns are just fiery tools in the service of ceramic art. The real thrill comes when you learn how to use them to create rich textures and colors on bisqued clay.

The book's co-authors, James and Paul, wanted to include the talents of several colleagues in clay at the mountaintop site of the photo shoot. These artists, who come from disparate areas of the United States, helped birth the beautiful work you'll see in this book. Don Ellis, long-time educator and potter from New Mexico, and Randy Brodnax, workshop showman and teacher from Texas, jammed kiln parts and pots and snack food into a truck and drove hundreds (and hundreds) of miles east. Linda Keleigh, a self-taught artist from New Jersey, piled barrels and wood and bisqued pots and mother-in-law into a van, then drove west (as did Paul). All the artists stayed and worked at the mountain home of Lark Books publisher Rob Pulleyn, himself a self-taught ceramist.

James, Paul, and crew show how to build a propane-fired raku kiln, and Randy contributes his nifty burner modification method to its design. Paul demonstrates a basic raku firing and sawdust reduction, how to pit-fire bisqued work, and how to clean and finish the fired pieces. James shares his techniques for obtaining silvery-black terra sigillata, iridescent luster fuming, low-temperature salt firing, and multi-colored surfaces. Don sets the world on fire with his copper glaze alcohol–reduction and horsehair processes. Linda Keleigh divulges how to burnish terra sigillata surfaces, and then how to create color in them with a wood-fired barrel. Randy shows how ferric chloride spices up raku glazes, plain bisqued pots, and aluminum foil saggar-fired work, then builds his own design for a downdraft-style barrel, complete with stovepipe chimney. And for the inaugural firing of Randy's kiln, all of us tried our hand at putting

colorants on the many pots that Randy had brought with him. Lark art director Kathy Holmes, photographer Evan Bracken (who celebrated his birthday during the shoot), and myself, the editor, ended up joining in the fun and work of demonstrating the fast-fire techniques and processes you'll see here. And throughout the book are many inspiring gallery images of raku-, pit-, and barrel-fired work by dozens of talented artists, some of whom contributed their firing secrets and glaze and slip recipes for you to use in your work. All of us sincerely hope you enjoy the results.

—*Suzanne Tourtillott*
Ceramics Editor

RAKU

RAKU

Raku is a popular low-temperature, fast-firing process that yields exciting, chance surface effects on ceramic ware. From a simple white crackle glaze to a surprising spectrum of color, from humble tea bowls to sculptural forms abstract or figurative, the range of possibility and innovation that resides in raku practice keeps it always young and vibrant. The modern Western practice of this ancient process, as well as its purpose, differs from its Eastern roots, but the results of raku are still infinite in their variety, energy, and beauty. Japanese and Western raku offer the ceramist the possibility of experiencing the final results of the firing in a relatively short time, and it is this very quality that makes the practice of raku so satisfying.

Origins and Modern Practice

The lineage of raku ware can be traced back 450 years, and many beautiful examples by the Raku family of Japan have been preserved at the Raku Museum in Kyoto. The word *raku* has been translated to mean ease, pleasure, or enjoyment, which epitomizes the state of being one attempts to achieve when engaging in the Japanese tea ceremony, or *chanoyu* ("the way of tea"). The technique of raku pottery originated in 16th-century Japan, during the Momoyama period, an era in which feudal warlords, or *shogun*, ruled with the aid of a militarily evolved and aesthetically conscious class of soldiers known as *samurai*. During this period a great tea master, Sen no Rikyu, acted as both the spiritual and social adviser to the exacting shogun society. Sen no Rikyu emphasized the *wabi* aesthetic, which stressed rusticity and simplicity in the tea ceremony and tearoom. He introduced the work of the potter Chojiro and his son, Jokei, to Toyotomi Hideyoshi, one of the dominant warlords of that time. It was Hideyoshi who bestowed, by means of a golden seal, the name Raku on Jokei, who first signed his wares with the Raku ideogram. The name continues to be passed down in this famous family of potters. It is evident in the work of each Raku descendant that he was able to express his individual aesthetic values, yet respect the principles of the tenets of the tea ceremony for which the wares were created.

Ron Boling
Walking Raku Bucket, 2002
27 x 13 x 13 in (69 x 33 x 33 cm); bisque
Δ 05 electric; Shiny Black/Copper Mist
glaze; propane fiber raku kiln; fired to
1,830°F (999°C); shredded paper reduction
Photo by John Hooper

There are differences between Japanese and Western raku method and philosophy. Japanese raku, for instance, refers only to pottery created by descendants of the Raku family for the traditional Japanese tea ceremony, which itself is a ritualistic endeavor. Traditional Japanese raku is not subjected to reduction materials after the ware has been taken out of the kiln. Western raku artists, by contrast, put the hot ware in contact with some sort of combustible material in a *reduction chamber* after removing it from the kiln. *Reduction* refers to a process whereby combustibles in contact with a hot piece burn, or reduce, the oxygen in the chamber, converting its atmosphere to one that's rich in carbon. Paul Soldner and other American artists pioneered this method in the early 1960s.

Western raku has evolved to encompass so many methods and materials that the results might better be described as post-fired reduction ware. This style of raku is free of the need to stay within the box of tradition and culture, and the no-holds-barred approach allows raku to be an evolving art form. The techniques illustrated in this section will act as a starting point for your own raku investigations, inevitably leading you to new and exciting discoveries.

**Black Raku Ware Tea Bowl, 1585–1589
Momoyama period (1568–1615),
Kyoto, Japan.
3¹/₃ x 4¹/₄ in (8.5 x 10.8 cm).
Pottery with black glaze; black
lacquer repairs**
Photo courtesy Arthur M. Sackler Gallery,
Smithsonian Institution, Washington, D.C.

**Linda Ganstrom
Seed Sisters, 2003
13 x 11 x 7 in (33 x 28 x 18 cm); Δ 07
electric, cooled to 1,200°F (649°C); air-
cooled until crackled, then newspaper
reduction in metal can**
Photo by Sheldon Ganstrom

Building a Raku Kiln

James Watkins, with some help from Randy Brodnax, demonstrates how to put together a propane-fired raku kiln. You can build one by yourself in a couple of hours or so. The finished kiln shown here is 24 inches (61 cm) tall and 24 inches (61 cm) in diameter, and it has a removable lid. It features some innovative design modifications that increase its efficiency, such as a baffle system and a modified burner orifice. (A popular alternative design joins the lid to the cylinder—often referred to as a "tophat" kiln—but to open it the entire affair must then be raised off its brick pad with a pulley-lift device.) James finds the former design to be equally effective and easier to build. It's nice to have an assistant remove the lid for you, though, so the work won't cool down too much before you can start the reduction process.

Be sure there is adequate space, clear of combustible materials, above and around the raku kiln. To protect the kiln from the weather, you might consider locating it under an open-sided shelter, with at least 8 feet (2.4 m) of clearance overhead so that smoke can escape.

Removing the ware from the kiln and placing it in the reduction chamber should be smooth and uninterrupted actions. Clear any objects that might intrude

A tophat raku kiln uses a pulley device to lift the firing chamber away from the kiln pad
Photo by Anna Vogler

into your path from kiln to reduction chamber before you start firing the kiln. Ideally, the reduction chamber should be close enough to the kiln so that it's possible to remove the ware and place it in the chamber in one easy step.

Position the propane gas tank at least 8 feet (2.4 m) away from the kiln, but keep it in sight of the burner port. Get the proper instruction from a technician or from the tank's manufacturer on how to make the connections, and be sure to check for gas leaks.

The fine particles in fiber blanket insulating material are a health and environmental hazard, particularly after the first firing. It's especially important that you wear a respirator fitted with the appropriate canisters and filters when you're handling the blanket material; don't expose your skin to the fibers, either. Consider using an improved blanket material, such as one made with the new soluble, high-temperature insulating fibers. You can find sources for it through a ceramics supply house or on the Internet.

Materials and Tools to Build a Raku Kiln

Most of the materials used for this lightweight kiln can be found at ceramic supply, industrial supply, and metal fabricators' shops. James doesn't recommend many substitutes. These materials were chosen for their strength and ability to withstand heat, or sometimes for safety reasons.

2 half-circle kiln shelves

16-gauge expanded metal with
1/2-inch (1.3 cm) openings,
4 x 8 feet (1.2 x 2.4 m) sheet

Lumber crayon

Heavy-duty wire cutters

1-inch (2.5 cm) insulation fiber
blanket, 6 pcf (96 kg/m³)

Permanent marker

Heavy-duty scissors

18-gauge nichrome

refractory wire

2 pairs of pliers

Twenty-four 2-part fiber anchor
pins, 2 inches (5 cm) long, rated
for a minimum of 2,100°F
(1,149°C); or 24 clay buttons

Utility knife

2 metal cabinet handles, with
bolts, washers, and nuts to
attach them

18 hard firebricks

22 soft firebricks, rated to
2,300°F (1,260°C)

Venturi burner capable of
producing 165,000 BTU with
propane or 60,000 BTU with
natural gas, with appropriate
hose fittings, high-pressure
regulator, and needle valve

Solder setup: solder, solder
paste, square of heavy-duty aluminum
foil, and soldering torch

Drill with 1/16-inch (1.6 mm)
bit for metal

Sandpaper

Plumber's tape

Wrench

80-gallon (360 L) propane tank,
with appropriate hose fittings

Ivory dishwashing liquid

1-inch (2.5 cm) hose, at least
8 feet (2.4 m) long

1 or 2 straight kiln shelves
and spacers

Hacksaw

Von Venhuizen
For Ages 2–4, 2003
15 x 10 x 10 in (38 x 25 x 25 cm);
gas fiber raku; 15 minutes in
newspaper and sawdust reduction
Photo by artist

Patrick Crabb
Shard teapot series, 1987
12 x 13 x 4 in
(31 x 33 x 10 cm);
gas raku kiln; reduction;
low-temperature salt
Photo by artist

Making the Chamber

Choose dry, level ground for the kiln site, whether it's concrete, asphalt, or hard earth. If the site is uneven use a shovel or spade to level the ground; for concrete or asphalt you'll have to level the bricks with sand. Check your work with a bubble level.

1. Gather together the materials for the kiln. The circumference of the cylinder for the chamber is based on the size of the kiln shelves you intend to use. The shelves should be able to accommodate your largest piece (photo 1). There must be 3 inches (7.6 cm) of space between the edges of the shelves and the kiln wall, so be sure to accurately calculate the length of expanded metal you'll need. The height of the kiln will be 24 inches (61 cm), which is equal to the standard width of fiber blanket.

2. Mark the sheet of expanded metal with a lumber crayon, and then cut it to the length you want with the wire cutters (photo 2).

3. Roll out the fiber blanket onto the cut piece of expanded metal. Mark and cut the blanket with the heavy-duty scissors so it matches the length of the metal (photo 3).

4. Bend the expanded metal into a cylinder (photo 4), overlapping the ends by a few inches.

5. Cut three short lengths of the nichrome wire. Use the pliers to twist the wire through the overlapped ends of the expanded metal, at the top, middle, and bottom of the cylinder's seam (photo 5).

6. Line the chamber with the fiber blanket (photo 6); it's okay if the fiber overlaps itself a bit. Align the ends of the blanket so they are over the metal seam.

7. Secure the fiber blanket to the chamber. If you're using the anchor pins, put a 3-inch (7.6 cm) square of fiber blanket between the stud and the ferrule (photo 7). You'll need two pairs of pliers to lock them together. Whichever type fasteners you use, position them every 12 inches (30.5 cm) or so around the top, the center, and the base of the chamber.

Charles and Linda Riggs
3 Naked Raku Pots, 2003
Left: 6¹/₂ x 5¹/₂ in.(17 x 14 cm);
Center: 7 x 5 in (18 x 13 cm);
Right: 5¹/₂ x 6¹/₄ in (14 x 16 cm);
dipped and polished terra
sigillata; tophat raku kiln; slip
resist ("naked raku") method
Photo by Charles Riggs

Cover the seam in the blanket with a 2-inch-wide (5 cm) strip of fiber blanket (photo 8).

8. Use scissors to cut a burner port or hole 2 inches (5 cm) from the bottom edge of the cylinder. The burner port should be 2 inches (2.5 cm) larger in diameter than the burner unit.

9. On the opposite side of the cylinder, midway up the wall, cut a peephole 3 inches (7.6 cm) in diameter.

10. The kiln lid's circumference should be slightly larger than the diameter of the cylinder (photo 9). Cut the expanded metal into a circle (photo 10), then cut a 3-inch (7.6 cm) flue hole in the center of it.

11. Place the lid on top of the fiber blanket. Since the lid is slightly larger than the maximum width of the blanket, cut two half-circles from the blanket. Use a utility knife to trim a

Ron Boling
Raku Straining Vessel, n.d.
10 x 31 in (25 x 79 cm); Δ 04
electric; copper glaze; propane
fiber raku kiln; fired to 1,830°F
(999°C); shredded paper reduction
Photo by John Hooper

ledge into the straight edge of one of the half-circles, so the two pieces can overlap, fitting neatly together (photo 11).

12. Attach the two handles to the lid, but closer to one edge rather than exactly flanking the flue hole (photo 12). Secure the fiber blanket to the lid as described in step 7. Cut the fiber blanket away from the flue hole.

13. Make a plug for the peephole out of fiber blanket. Cut the fiber 4 inches (10.2 cm) wide. Determine the length by rolling it up until it's big enough to fill the peephole (photo 13). Wrap the fiber plug with refractory wire near each edge and in the center. Cut and flatten the wire's ends so they won't catch on the edges of the peephole.

Laying the Pad

On level ground, build a kiln pad with two layers of refractory brick. The dimensions of the kiln pad need be only large enough to accommodate the circumference of the kiln. Lay the bottom layer of the pad with hard firebrick in a pattern similar to photo 14. Stagger a second layer of soft brick over the first one (photo 15).

The venturi burner receives propane gas through a hose connected to the tank, mixing the gas with oxygen in varying proportions depending on the position of the intake valve and the size of the burner's orifice.

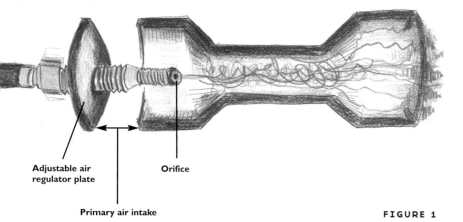

Adjustable air regulator plate

Orifice

Primary air intake

FIGURE 1

Setting Up the Burner

1. The venturi burner is designed to mix air and gas (figure 1). Be sure to ask your gas supplier for the appropriate hose, orifice (natural or propane), and needle valve (see figure 2) when you buy the burner. If you use natural gas, you won't need to modify the burner orifice at all, so you should skip steps 1 through 4. For propane, though, you'll first need to make the burner's orifice smaller so that it can control the flow of the gas more efficiently.

The needle valve is positioned between the pressure regulator and the venturi burner.

FIGURE 2

2. Disassemble the burner and remove the orifice.

3. Set up to solder: place a small piece of silver solder, coated with solder paste, into the bowl of the orifice, and set it on a square of heavy-duty aluminum foil that sits on a firebrick (photo 16). Try to use just enough solder to fill the area without over-running it. Warm the solder with a soldering torch, then melt it (photo 17).

4. Drill a new hole, $^{1}/_{16}$ inch (1.6 mm) in diameter, through the center of the orifice. Sand off any excess solder that protrudes beyond the orifice's edge (photo 18).

5. Reassemble the burner. First wrap the end of the hose with a short piece of plumber's tape, then use a wrench to attach the hose to the burner's fitting. Make sure it's a tight fit. Follow the same procedure to fit the hose to the propane tank, fitting the needle valve to the high-pressure regulator.

6. Do a leak test for each connection. Spray a weak mixture of Ivory dishwashing liquid and water (only a soap without a petroleum base, such as Ivory brand soap, may be used for this test; others may spontaneously combust!) on all the connections for both oxygen and propane. If bubbles appear around these connections, tighten them more and spray again. Propane has a marker odor added to it so you'll know if it's leaking, but test it carefully each time you change the connections.

Assembling the Kiln

1. Arrange refractory bricks in an open circle in the center of the kiln pad. Leave an opening at the burner side. The brick directly opposite the burner port is the target brick that will redirect the propane flame (see figure 3).

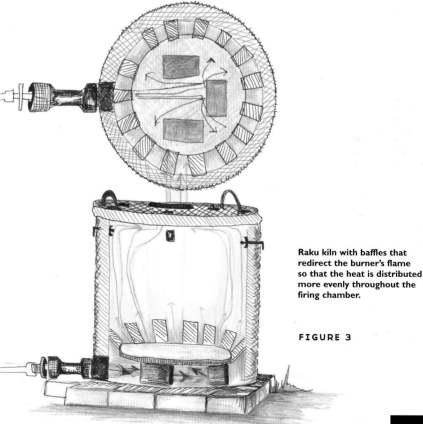

Raku kiln with baffles that redirect the burner's flame so that the heat is distributed more evenly throughout the firing chamber.

FIGURE 3

Piero Fenci
Origami with Blue Eyes, 2002
18 x 18 x 14 in (46 x 46 x 36 cm);
brick top-load kiln; fired to 1,850°F
(1,010°C); brief reduction in wet hay
Photo by Harrison Evans

the circular shelves so they create a baffle (photo 22).

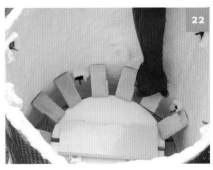

2. Lay the two half-circle kiln shelves onto the brick circle (photo 19). Place a straight kiln shelf (or two if the base of your piece is wide) on top of several spacers (photo 20).

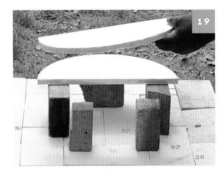

3. Set the chamber onto the kiln pad.

4. Use the hacksaw to cut several soft firebricks lengthwise into 1-inch-wide (2.5 cm) pieces (photo 21). Arrange these all around the edges of

5. Build a pad for the burner from additional firebricks, so that it clears the bottom of the burner port. Lay the burner onto a piece of fiber blanket 1 inch (2.5 cm) from the edge of the kiln chamber's outer wall (photo 23). The front edge of the burner should be positioned just at the edge of the port. If the burner extends too far into the firing chamber there won't be a good mixture of fuel and oxygen.

Basic Raku Firing

For the reduction container, use a large metal trashcan with a tight-fitting lid. For this and all of the other firing processes described in this book, be sure to wear heat-resistant gloves and sleeves, and a heat-resistant, protective apron (photo 24). Don't stare at the glowing ware for long periods without eye protection, either (it's been proven to cause long-term retinal damage). James recommends using welder's safety glasses, preferably those with didymium lenses. Use raku tongs to remove the ware. Be sure to use a properly fitted and filtered air-purifying respirator when smoke, vapors, or gasses are present—even outdoors.

Clay bodies with somewhat more grog are better able to handle the stresses of *thermal shock*. Be sure to use well-wedged clay to avoid the air pockets that could cause the ware to break during the firing. Apply a white crackle raku glaze

(see the recipe in the sidebar) to a bisqued pot. The earliest glazes developed in the Near East were also alkaline glazes. These glazes have the effect of heightening the color reaction to oxides but also have a tendency to craze, making them unsafe for functional ware. However, they are suitable for raku and other decorative ware because they create beautiful crackled surfaces. Once you've explored the basic fast-firing and reduction procedure, the exciting world of raku surfaces opens to your imagination.

This glaze has a relatively low percentage of oxide added to its base recipe. Glazes with a higher percentage of oxide will create lustrous, iridescent surface colors, and flame patterns will be traced on the ware's surface. The thinner this glaze is applied, the smaller the crackle pattern (platelets) will be. See the Glazes and Slips section (pages 118–119) for more raku glaze recipes.

You can also add colorants to a basic white raku crackle glaze. To create blue in this base glaze formula, Randy Brodnax recommends adding .5 percent cobalt oxide; use 5 percent copper carbonate for a lustrous copper-penny color.

Reg Brown
Stolen Generations, 2002
13 x 10 x 10 in (33 x 25 x 25 cm);
burnished stoneware; poured lithium
slip with white crackle glaze
teardrops; propane, fiber oil-drum
raku kiln; newspaper reduction
Photo by Tommy Elder

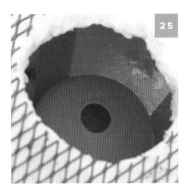

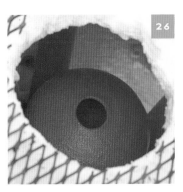

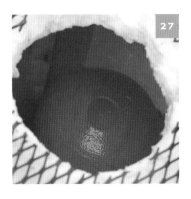

White crackle glaze, raku-fired with sawdust reduction by Paul Andrew Wandless.

How to Fire

Here's where it gets exciting. In the raku kiln you just built, you'll quickly bring the glazed pot up to temperature, then plunge the hot ware into a container that holds sawdust or some other combustible material, producing a carbonaceous reduction atmosphere. This atmosphere affects unglazed clay and the surface crazing in glazes, staining them a rich black.

There are three ways to determine if a glossy glaze is mature. You may read the kiln's temperature from a pyrometer, check the slump of a pyrometric cone, or evaluate the glaze by its surface appearance. Before the glaze has reached the correct temperature, it will have a matte look (photo 25). As it approaches maturity, beads of "sweat" appear (photo 26). The glaze is mature when the beading flattens out; the surface will look very smooth and glossy (photo 27). For matte glazes, which don't shine when they reach maturity, use a pyrometer or pyrometric cone. Before you fire, build up some firebricks inside the kiln to the level of the peephole, so you can use cones instead.

Caution: When you're using sawdust for reduction, use a heavier rather than a lighter grade. Very fine sawdust will explode if poured on top of hot ware.

Copper Wash
Fire to 1,850°F (1,010°C). The surface will be somewhat smoother than when it's fired to lower temperatures.

37.5	Copper carbonate
37.5	Black copper oxide
12.5	Frit 3110
8.3	Red iron oxide
4.2	Cobalt carbonate
100.0	Total

1. Check that the position of the burner's air regulator plate (refer to figure 1 on page 22) is halfway open. Insert the pyrometer's probe into the peephole (photo 28).

2. Place 2 inches (5 cm) of sawdust into the trashcan, and have plenty more nearby in a large, light container that is easy to pick up. Load the kiln (photo 29).

3. Check that the tank's main supply valve is open but the needle valve is closed. If you're alone, you'll use a propane torch (such as the one you used to solder the orifice) to light the burner. Lay the torch on its side so that the flame from it will pass straight across (in front of) the burner. Light the torch and then go to the tank. Remember, leave the burner on its pad while you stand at the tank! Slowly open the needle

valve, just until the gas ignites at the burner. Turn off the torch and remove it from the burner area. If you have a helper, so much the better. (In addition to the instructions here, be sure to review the manufacturer's information.)

4. Bring the kiln's temperature up in three stages, each stage lasting 20 minutes.

Stage 1: Let the burner operate at the flow that was needed to light it; if necessary, adjust the regulator plate so that there's a licking flame and a soft hissing sound as the fuel and oxygen are mixed.

Stage 2: Increase the flow of the propane so that the flame becomes longer and stronger. There should be a roaring sound as the propane and oxygen mix, and soon the interior of the kiln will begin to turn red.

Stage 3: Increase the fuel flow slightly, adjusting it just enough to get the pyrometer's readout up to the desired glaze temperature. (If you're using pyrometric cones, you'll have to learn how much more to increase the fuel flow through trial and error, or you can judge that you've reached the desired temperature visually, as described on page 27.) When the glaze has matured, use tongs to remove the ware from the kiln (photo 30).

5. Place the piece inside the reduction container and cover it with organic material such as sawdust. The fuel ignites immediately on contact. Quickly pour more sawdust over the ware to smother the fire.

6. Remove the ware when the container has cooled (photo 31). Use a nylon scrubbing pad to clean the ash from the surface (photo 32).

TIP

For subtle textural effects on raku use a copper wash on bisque ware (see sidebar on page 28). Experiment with different combustible materials, such as dried flowers, pine needles, and straw. Each organic substance yields its own spectrum of dramatic colors and textures as it interacts with the copper, iron, and cobalt in the wash.

Alternative Raku Reduction Techniques

In the West, the raku process is practically synonymous with creative experimentation in reduction. Here are seven alternatives that will give you interesting fast-fire surface effects.

White crackle glaze fumed with ferric chloride solution and raku-fired by Randy Brodnax.

Amber-Tinted Ferric Chloride Reduction

Ferric chloride is an iron solution that colors raku-fired ware and raku glazes with tones of rust and amber, adding luster to a glazed surface without changing the glaze's basic characteristic, whether it's crackled, textured, or a fully

Richard Hirsch
Altar Bowl #30, 2001
14¹/₂ x 16 in (37 x 41 cm);
**polychrome terra sigillatas under
low-fire glazes; multi-fired in fiber
raku kiln; fumed with ferric chloride
or cupric sulfate**
Photo by Geoff Tesch

opaque one. The greatest degree of iridescence is obtained with light applications over the lightest glaze colors; fewer layers of chemical are needed over darker glazes. Randy Brodnax applies the solution over colored raku glazes to introduce varying degrees of iridescence to them, and shows how to create smoked reduction with a simple newspaper technique.

Ferric chloride solution, also called copper etchant, is corrosive to eyes, skin, and lungs. Handle it with respect, and follow the manufacturer's recommendations for its use and storage. You can obtain the Materials Safety Data Sheet (MSDS) for this product on the Internet, or contact the manufacturer.

White crackle glazes work very well for this process, but each glaze will react differently to the solution and how heavily or lightly it's applied. Experiment with the application of the solution to discover what visual effect you enjoy most. The more you work with this process the more control you'll gain over the colors you create. Raku glazes are listed in the Glazes, Slips, and Colorants section on pages 118–119.

Materials and Tools

Bisque ware

Stand or stool

Metal banding wheel

2 soft firebricks

Newspaper

Large, heavy towel
saturated in water

Tongs

Ferric chloride solution
(2 tablespoons [30 mL] in
8 ounces [240 mL] water)

2-piece disposable spray
gun with refillable
container and
propellant, available at
hardware stores, for the
ferric chloride

Soft cloth

Instructions

Caution: When removing ware from the kiln or spraying the ferric chloride solution, be sure to wear your protective gear, including a respirator, arm shields, and heat-resistant gloves.

1. Place the stand near the kiln and put the banding wheel on it. Set the firebricks on the wheel; the firebricks act as insulators to keep the ware from cooling too fast at its base. Place several sheets of the newspaper, 5 to 6 inches (12.7–15.2 cm) wider than the dimensions of the ware, on the ground. Have more newspaper and the water-soaked towel close by.

2. Fire the glazed ware in the raku kiln to the melting range of the applied glaze. Once it's hot enough, use the tongs to move the ware from the kiln to the firebricks on the banding wheel. The ware's temperature should be about 1,700°F (927°C) when you remove it from the kiln.

3. Spin the banding wheel and evenly spray the ferric chloride onto the hot ware (photo 33), holding it 4 to 5 inches (10.2–12.7 cm) from the surface. Right away you'll see the ferric chloride start to darken and develop rusty hues on the surface. The hotter the ware, the darker the resulting

color. As the ware cools during the spraying, colors may range from dark amber to orange then to yellow. Continue the process until you see the colors you desire, for a maximum of 1 minute. The ware must remain hot (1,500–1,100°F [816–593°C]) for the next step.

4. When you're finished spraying the ferric chloride, it's safe to remove your respirator. Use the tongs to place the hot ware on top of the newspaper (photo 34) and place two to four sheets of newspaper on top of it, stepping back right away from the flames (photo 35). The newspaper will burn away quickly, and the smoke will turn the clay body dark, creating a crackled effect on the glazed ware. Allow the paper to burn on the surface for a few minutes. As it turns to ash and exposes some parts of the ware, quickly place a new piece of newspaper on top of the ware, then drape the towel over the entire piece (photo 36) to extinguish the fire and quickly cool the ware. (The towel will smoke, but it won't catch fire.)

Richard Hirsch
Altar Bowl #20, 2001
14 x 19^1/$_2$ x 8^1/$_2$ in (36 x 50 x 22 cm);
polychrome terra sigillatas under low-
fire glazes; multi-fired in fiber raku kiln;
fumed with ferric chloride
Photo by Geoff Tesch

5. After a few minutes you may remove the towel and let the ware continue to cool on its own (photo 37).

6. When the ware is completely cooled, wipe the surface with a soft cloth.

Horsehair reduction on bisque ware by Don Ellis.

High-Contrast Horsehair Reduction

Don Ellis demonstrates how a simple horsehair reduction technique gets visually dramatic results on a pot that was bisqued with buffed terra sigillata. The process creates a particularly striking contrast of black and white in bold, minimalist patterns. Horsehair burning on the surface creates local reduction in the immediate area it's in contact with, and the carbon that the hair leaves behind enables you to "draw" directly onto the surface, producing strong black lines with light carbon trails of gray that accent the movements of your design.

The basic horsehair process can be done on any bisqued piece, such as one coated with porcelain slip, or on bisqued porcelain ware. Before you begin, put the banding wheel and horsehair on a stand or table near the kiln. If you don't have a raku kiln, you can pull the work from an electric kiln instead. Burning horsehair produces very little smoke, so you can even work inside if you don't mind the smell of burning hair.

Instructions

1. Place the stand near the kiln and put the banding wheel on it. Set the firebricks on the wheel; these will act as insulators to keep the ware from cooling too fast at its base.

2. Load the ware onto a shelf so that the top of the piece is 6 inches (15.2 cm) from the lid and directly below the flu hole. For smaller pieces you may need to elevate your kiln shelves with soft brick. When the temperature reaches 1,700°F (927°C), check the surface to see if it's ready. Through the flu hole, drop a few granules of sugar onto the ware. If the sugar burns off immediately, leaving black specks, the work is ready to be removed (photo 38). Let the black specks burn away completely before removing the work; this will take only a few seconds more.

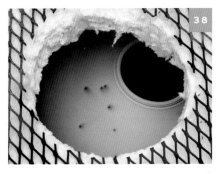

3. Remove the ware with tongs and place it on the metal banding wheel. Put the tongs aside and remove your gloves, but keep the facemask on, since there will be some smoke coming off the surface. The smoke isn't toxic, but the horsehair has a pungent smell.

4. Drape the horsehair on the ware, holding it at each end to pull it straight and laying it on the shoulder of the ware (photo 39). As the hair burns on the surface the smoke creates a softly graduated gray carbon trail in the direction of the airflow. To create irregular lines, hold some horsehair (either one or a clump of it) by one end and lay it on the surface (photo 40).

5. Sprinkle a few grains of sugar on the surface (photo 41), laying it down in a pattern or just turning the banding wheel, depending on what your design may be.

6. Drop a wad of tissues inside the pot (photo 42) to make it turn black. Once the pot has completely cooled, use a soft cloth to wipe off any ashes.

Materials and Tools

Horsehair is available from any horse stable or handy barbed-wire range fence, or you can find it in a western-gear shop that carries horsehair for craft projects.

Bisque ware, with or without terra sigillata

Stand or stool

Metal banding wheel

2 soft firebricks

Granulated sugar

Tongs

Horsehair

Facial tissue

Soft cloth

Horsehair and feather reduction (sprayed with ferric chloride) on bisque ware by Randy Brodnax.

Rust-Red Reduction

Randy Brodnax likes to experiment with different materials for a loose and spontaneous effect on his work. Here he gets quick effects in the open air by employing some of the same techniques used in the ferric chloride and horsehair reduction processes. Multiple applications result in a rusty red-brown effect, sometimes ranging to black, on an unglazed surface. Experiment with the application of ferric chloride, keeping in mind that all glazes react differently to the ferric chloride solution. Other kinds of organic materials, such as twigs, leaves, and flowers, will burn nicely on the surface of the hot ware, and the local reduction will create beautiful and distinct patterns.

Be sure to wear a respirator fitted with canisters and filters that are appropriate for the vapors created by the solution as it burns. Review the safety notes from the Amber-Tinted Ferric Chloride Reduction process (page 31) for important information about the materials, tools, and safety considerations related to using ferric chloride.

Instructions

1. From the horsehair reduction technique, follow the directions for steps 1 and 2. To smoke the bottom of the hot pot, lay a paper towel on the banding wheel before setting it there. Sprinkle some sugar over the pot (photo 43).

2. Use pliers to place the feathers onto the hot pot (photo 44). Apply the horsehair (photo 45), as described in step 4 on page 35.

3. Spray the ferric chloride on the surface (photo 46). The heavier the application of the solution, the darker the effect will be. Spray the whole pot, or do smaller areas.

4. Drop a facial tissue into the pot to create a smoky finish inside it (photo 47).

5. Pour a cup of water on the ware to quickly cool it.

Materials and Tools

Bisque ware with raku glaze

Paper towel

Metal banding wheel

Granulated sugar

Pliers

Feathers

Horsehair

2 firebricks

2-piece disposable spray gun with refillable container and propellant, available at hardware stores, for the ferric chloride

Ferric chloride solution

Facial tissue

Cup of water

Terra Sigillata Reduction

Terra sigillata is a type of slip made with clays whose particles are extremely fine. The material is very versatile in how it can be applied, and it bonds extremely well to the surface of the clay body. The high ratio of water to clay in the recipe given here creates a slip that works on both bisque and green ware. Apply it with a brush or airbrush, pour it over a surface, or even dip the ware into it. After the sigillata dries you can burnish it (on green ware) or buff it (on bisque) to create a silky, lustrous appearance.

Origins of Terra Sigillata

Terra sigillata is Latin for "sealed earth." For thousands of years, terra sigillata has been used as a sealer or a decorative coat on pottery. Earliest examples of this are red-black classical Greek pottery, rich red Roman pottery, and in North America, burnished black pottery of Native Americans. The Roman ware was covered with a red slip/terra sigillata and fired in oxidation, creating a rich red color. This method was used in Italy and other areas of the Roman Empire as well as in pre-Columbian and South American cultures.

Greek pottery is unique for its black and red terra sigillata surfaces. After the terra sigillata turned black in a reduction atmosphere, the makers reoxidized the kiln atmosphere at the end of the firing. The areas of the pot without the sigillata reverted back to the red of the clay body. Since the clay pottery and the terra sigillata were made from the same red clay, they were able to obtain results that were very consistent and repeatable.

Bacia Edelman
Sphere with Blade Top (vase), n.d.
18 x 14 x 14 in (46 x 36 x 36 cm); bisque
Δ 010 electric; airbrushed terra sigillata;
straw and sawdust reduction in oil drum
drilled with airholes
Photo by artist

Making the Terra Sigillata

Once it's mixed, the terra sigillata will need to sit, undisturbed, for some time (opinions vary widely as to how long is necessary). It will precipitate into three distinct layers: water, terra sigillata, and a bottom layer made up of larger, heavier clay particles, of which only the sigillata will be useful.

Blender
1-gallon (3.8 L) clear glass or
plastic jar with lid
2 bowls
Clear tubing

1. Thoroughly mix the ball clay, EPK, and water in a blender.

2. Add the sodium silicate, one drop at a time. Transfer the mixture to the jar and cover it. Let it sit for four days.

3. Arrange the jar so that its base stands above the level of the rims of your two empty bowls, being careful not to disturb the jar's contents (photo 48).

4. Fill the tubing with clean water and cover each end with your thumbs. Gently lower one end about midway into the top layer of the jar and uncover that end of the tube. Position the other end over one of the bowls and remove your thumb from it. Once the top layer has moved into the first bowl, move the tube end into the second bowl (photo 49). The terra sigillata solution will be very thin. Discard the bottom layer of clay.

RECIPE

*Terra Sigillata #1
for Bisque or Green Ware*

1½ cups (205.5 g) ball clay
1½ cups (172.5 g) EPK clay
10 cups (2.4 L) water
2 tablespoons (30 mL) sodium silicate

Gunmetal Black Reduction

For this raku firing process, terra sigillata is applied to bisque ware. The dried organic matter used for the reduction produces a very rich, unglazed gunmetal-black surface that picks up traces of its texture and shape.

How to Fire

1. Apply a thin, light coat of terra sigillata to the ware with a brush (see photo 50) or spray it on with a sprayer (see photo 51). A too-thick application will flake off after firing. Lightly buff the ware with a soft cloth or chamois until it shines (photo 52). If you prefer a satin finish, don't buff it.

2. Place 2 inches (5 cm) of sawdust, or any other organic material, in the trash can. The terra sigillata will pick up the texture of the reduction material.

3. Fire the ware in the kiln (photo 53). The terra sigillata matures between 1,700° and 1,850°F (927–1,010°C).

4. Use tongs to remove the ware from the kiln and place it into the trash can (photo 54); the sawdust will ignite. Cover the ware with more sawdust (photo 55) and put on the lid (photo 56).

5. Leave the ware in the trash can until the can is cool to the touch (photo 57), then clean off the ash.

Materials and Tools

Bisque ware

Terra sigillata

Hake brush or spray apparatus

Soft cloth or chamois

Sawdust or other organic materials

Metal trash can with tight-fitting lid

Tongs

**Copper matte–alcohol reduction
on bisque ware by Don Ellis.**

Materials and Tools

Stainless-steel bowl

Large metal washtub or
other suitable container

Playground sand, enough
to fill the container

Heat-resistant glass bowl

Pine needles

Copper Matte–Alcohol Reduction

For this particularly dramatic reduction technique, Don Ellis sprays rubbing alcohol on the hot surface of ware that has been fired with a copper wash. As the alcohol burns off in a reduction atmosphere, brilliant, colorful patterns appear. Don uses an ingenious reduction chamber that lets him keep an eye on the surface color as it changes so he can pull the piece from it and fix the rapidly changing glaze colors with water at just the right moment.

Don recommends only one brand of sealer, Jasco Silicone Grout Sealer. It effectively protects the copper from *reoxidization* (tarnishing) due to exposure to oxygen and dirt. To further ensure the copper's stability, clean the outside of the pot by spritzing it with plain water every six months or so.

Setting Up the Chamber

The reduction chamber consists of two parts: a stainless-steel bowl sunk into a tub full of sand and a see-through cover (see figure 4), which should be proportionate to the size of the piece you intend to fire. Several cover sizes and designs are shown in photo 58. For a small piece, a clear bowl made of tempered glass works well. For larger pieces, adhere a larger bowl to a washtub or a fired-clay collar with high-temperature automotive gasket sealant.

The sand should come right up to the rim of the stainless-steel bowl; there should also be a few inches under it. The sand acts as an insulator to keep the temperature inside the bowl from falling too quickly. Also place a few inches of sand in the bottom of the metal bowl to shield the hot ware from thermal shock and to give it a stable base. Add about a dozen pine needles, which will leave interesting patterns on the bottom of the work and also help to consume the oxygen in the container as they combust on contact (photo 59).

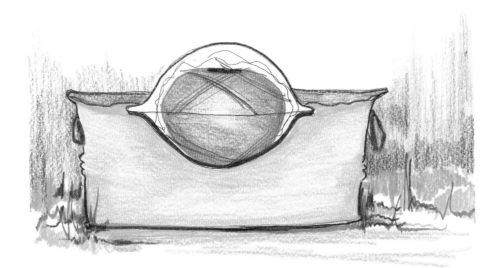

Figure 4. An ingenious reduction chamber constructed of a tempered-glass bowl inverted over a steel one, which is sunk into a bed of sand.

FIGURE 4

Nicole Dezelon
Tall Bottle (1 & 2), 2002
17 x 5¹/₂ x 3 in (43 x 14 x 8 cm);
eggshell raku, copper red glazes, and wax
resist; reduction cooled to Δ 07; reduced
in metal can
Photo by artist

How to Fire

It's important that your movements
from the kiln to the banding wheel to
the reduction chamber are smooth
and quick throughout this process, so
prepare everything in advance. You
might even want to practice your
movements with a helper beforehand.

1. Spray the copper wash to a moder-
ate thickness onto a bisqued piece. If
the wash is applied too heavily the
piece will have a scaly surface.

2. Fire the ware to 1,750°F (954°C).
Copper washes have a dark, matte
appearance in the kiln, so use a
pyrometer or pyrometric cone, rather
than a visual assessment, to determine its maturity. Place the banding
wheel on a stand or stool. Remove the
work with tongs (photo 60) and place
it immediately on the banding wheel.

3. Slowly turn the wheel as you apply
an even coat of the rubbing alcohol
with the garden sprayer. It's important to keep the ware turning as you
spray it. This allows for an even coat
around the entire surface.

Caution: When the alcohol hits the
surface, flames will leap off the work
as it burns off (photo 61). Stay an
arm's length away and don't lean
forward. As the alcohol burns off,
copper coloration will appear
momentarily on the surface before it
turns black again.

4. Repeat the spraying process several
times, waiting 5 seconds between each
spraying. Each time you spray you'll
see a colorful ring appear, then disap-
pear, around the ware: at first it will be
red, then blue, and finally purple.
Keep turning the ware as you build up
the alcohol application. After six to
nine layers, a purple ring or halo will
appear in each sprayed area. You've
applied enough alcohol.

5. Use the tongs to place the ware in the steel bowl. Place one dozen or so pine needles on top of the ware and allow them to burn for a moment (photo 62). Place the bowl on top of the ware and quickly make a tight seal by covering the edges with sand where the two bowls meet (photo 63).

6. After 10 to 12 seconds, as the oxygen is consumed, the entire work begins to turn a copper color. After 1 minute, when the ware is completely copper colored, lift one edge of the cover a bit and quickly spray alcohol into the chamber, then, just as quickly, drop the cover and bury its edge with sand again. As the alcohol burns away, the reds, blues, and purples will reappear on the ware's surface (photo 64).

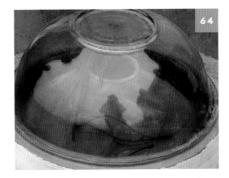

7. Once the ware has cooled a bit (8 to 9 minutes for a smaller piece or 13 to 14 minutes for a larger one) you can attempt to control the color patterns by very briefly lifting ("burping") the cover to allow a little air inside. A colorful pattern will appear on the side opposite where the air entered the chamber. If the ware has cooled just the right amount, you'll see the orange-to-violet range of colors slowly begin to appear on the surface; this is the result of reoxidization. If it's too hot, the ware will quickly turn yellow. If allowed to cool too much, the piece will stay copper colored or turn somewhat orange with only a hint of violet.

8. Remove the ware with tongs and place it back on the metal turntable. Immediately spray it with water to set the colors (photo 65).

9. After the ware has cooled, use the tile sealant so that the colorful surface will have greater longevity.

RECIPE

Copper Wash for Alcohol Reduction
Fire to 1,750°F (954°C). The surface will be somewhat rougher than when it's fired to higher temperatures.

36.0	Copper carbonate
36.0	Black copper oxide
16.0	Frit 3110
8.0	Red iron oxide
4.0	Cobalt carbonate
100.0	Total

Materials and Tools

Bisque ware

Copper wash glaze (see sidebar)

Glaze spray apparatus

Pyrometer or 06 cones

Tongs

Metal banding wheel

Stand or stool

Pump-style garden sprayer, available at home improvement centers*

91% rubbing alcohol

Sprayer bottle with water

Jasco Ceramic Tile Silicon Grout Sealer

Only this type of sprayer will deliver enough pressure to be able to spray the ware quickly enough.

Fumed with stannous chloride and wire stencils on bisque ware by James C. Watkins.

Iridescent Luster Fuming

Fuming is a vapor-glazing technique whereby stannous chloride (also called tin chloride), a metallic salt, is introduced into the kiln at dull heat to create swirls of iridescent markings. Colorful rainbow glazes have always been very popular, and the technique of fuming provides brilliant archival colors that won't fade with time. The fuming technique has its origins in glassblowing, in which metallic salts are used to create lustrous mother-of-pearl effects on glass surfaces. In 1969 clay artist Biz Littell began experimenting with fuming using stannous chloride. His fumed applications of gold, platinum, and other precious-metal lusters on clay were christened "Kosai ware" (from the Japanese ideogram "hue of light") by Japanese artist Chyako Hashimoto.

James demonstrates how to fume in a raku kiln, on ware that was fired with a commercial metallic glaze. Applying a precious-metal luster to a metallic-glazed piece enhances the rainbow coloration, creating an even greater range of color and depth to the fumed surface than does stannous chloride alone. If you'd like a less glossy glaze than the one shown here, use one of Biz Littell's fuming glaze recipes from the Glazes, Slips, and Colorants appendix on page 119. The vessel on page 65 shows the glossy metallic glaze in a central motif, surrounded by Biz's satin formula, and fumed in a clay saggar.

The fuming process requires that you employ precautionary safeguards related to using hazardous chemicals, and this advice is especially true when using metallic salts, which are highly toxic. Be sure to wear a respirator fitted with the appropriate acid gas cartridges; never work indoors with it. Fuming is worthy of the effort, though; beautiful, permanent results can capture all the colors of the rainbow.

Fuming in a Raku Kiln

1. Fire the ware to the glaze's maturity (cone 04), then let it cool completely. (If you don't intend to use the luster or the wire stencils, let the ware cool to 800 to 900°F [427–482°C], and proceed to step 5.) Be sure to check the temperature with a pyrometer.

2. Use bailing wire to create a stenciled surface on the ware. Cut the wire and shape it into designs of your choosing. Place these designs on the surface of the glazed and fired ware (photo 66). Bailing wire will not burn away at cone 019, which is the firing range of both gold and platinum lusters.

3. Use an atomizer to spray the luster onto the ware (photo 67).

4. Load the ware into the kiln. Place the firebricks opposite each other in the kiln. Fire the ware to cone 019, then let it cool to 800 to 900°F (427–482°C).

5. Remove the lid from the top of the kiln. Pour the stannous chloride onto the two hot firebricks (photo 68 on page 48). The stannous chloride will vaporize on contact with the hot clay, emitting the vapor that creates a rainbow effect on the surface of the ware. Too much will create a cloudy white film. Replace the kiln lid.

Materials and Tools

Bisque-fired ware

Duncan SY 553 Antique Brass glaze

Pyrometer

Bailing wire

Wire cutters

019 cone

Atomizer

Gold or platinum luster (optional)

Tongs

2 hard firebricks

3 tablespoons (55 g) stannous chloride in a small plastic cup

Biz Littell
Autumn Mist Series, 1999
18 x 10¹/₂ x 10¹/₂ in (46 x 27 x 27 cm);
gold luster–fumed Kosai ware
Photo by artist

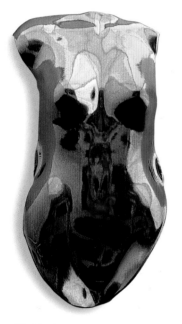

Biz Littell
Platinum Nude, n.d.
32 x 18 x 10 in (81 x 46 x 25 cm);
gold luster–fumed Kosai ware
Photo by artist

6. One minute after the stannous chloride has been introduced into the kiln, partially open the lid to release the fumes (photo 69). It will take about 1 minute for the kiln to clear. Close the lid and allow the kiln to cool completely. The rainbow effect will be immediately apparent (photo 70).

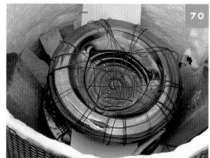

TIPS

Stannous chloride is moderately corrosive, but James says he's used the fuming technique in an electric kiln for two years without any noticeable damage to the elements.

Fuming may also be done in a bed of sand. Once the ware and the hot bricks are at the right temperature, take them out of the kiln and place them on the sand. Sprinkle the stannous chloride onto the hot bricks, then cover the whole affair with a metal or clay container. Finish the process as described above.

After adding the stannous chloride and airing the kiln, you can experiment with postfired reduction by covering still-hot ware with dry organic materials. This will turn any unglazed parts of the clay dark.

Low-Fire Salt Fuming

While James was giving a slide lecture in Beijing, China, a student asked him what were the similarities between low-fire salt and Western-style raku. His response was that both techniques use organic materials and they both provide an unlimited range of possible textures and colors. Another shared phenomenon is the happy accidents that can occur during the firing. The low-fire salt technique uses a variety of salt-laden organic materials, which create strong, warm colors that appear to

James C. Watkins
Double-Walled Bowl
(from the *Guardian* series), 2003
9 x 19 in (22.9 x 48.3 cm);
buffed terra sigillata; fired to ∆ 022,
(1,166°F [630°C]) in foil saggar with
copper sulfate–soaked Spanish moss
and table salt
Photo by Hershel Womack

overlap each other. This overlapping effect on the surface can create great visual depth that sometimes results in work that can surpass one's own aesthetic sensibilities. Inherent in both raku and low-fire salt is the possibility for continued invention and discovery.

The high-temperature salt-firing process originated in Germany during the 12th century. High-fire salt glazing introduces loose salt into openings in the kiln during a late stage of the firing. The salt vaporizes immediately on contact with the intense heat, creating a thin glaze on the ware. Some modern high-fire Japanese Bizen wares are draped in seaweed or wrapped in rope that has been soaked in salt water, then fired in a wood kiln. The sodium-laden ashes combine with the silica in the clay to create beautiful flashes of warm colors in organic patterns.

The low-fire salt process is done in a simple brick enclosure, which is built inside the raku kiln, and fired between 1,616 and 1,958°F (880–1,070°C). This is considerably lower than the temperatures used for either high-fire salt or Bizen ware. If the ware is fired to a temperature lower than cone 012, the salt will not

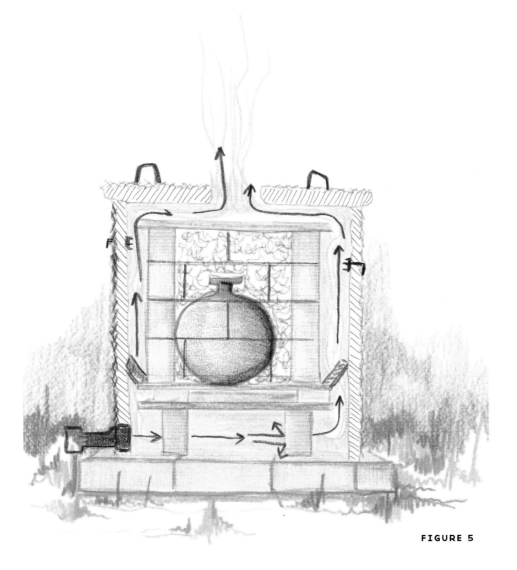

FIGURE 5

The raku kiln's firing chamber can hold a loose-brick saggar for low-fire salt fuming.

vaporize. If the ware is fired to temperatures higher than cone 04, it will turn a single shade of dark brown. To get the best results from the salt-laden materials they must be in close contact with the ware. This can be quite a challenge. One way is to wrap the ware in chicken wire or ceramic fiber so that the organic material hugs it.

A large range of surfacing techniques can be experimented with when firing low-fire salt. Simply paint or spray slips, terra sigillata, or underglazes on the clay body before the bisque firing. Salts and oxides will reward you with an array of color flashes. These materials can be applied to the bisqued pieces in several ways: sprayed, daubed, painted, sprinkled around the ware, or pressed into pads of clay and laid directly on the ware. Copper sulfate is a naturally occurring inorganic salt and, like table salt and other salts, it will produce warm colors ranging from pink to yellow to orange. Some other materials that have proven to be successful are rock salt, Epsom salt, lithium (which is also a salt), high-potassium plant foods, garden fertilizers, copper carbonate, copper sulfate, and zinc granules. To cultivate a stratum of colors, try organic or commercial materials, such as seaweed, banana skins,

Materials and Tools

Bisque ware

Firebrick

Hardwood pieces,
2 x 2 inches (5.1 x 5.1 cm)

1 1/2 cups (300 g)
table salt

Ferric chloride (review
the safety notes on page 31)

Copper carbonate

Wet-clay collar, 1/8 inch
(3 mm) thick

Sawdust, straw, and
vermiculite, soaked in salt
water and dried*

2 straight kiln shelves

*All materials should be thoroughly
dry before coming into contact with
the ware. Any salt water absorbed
into the clay body will expand,
causing sheets of the clay to peel off
if later exposed to a wet atmosphere
(because the firing doesn't reach
temperatures high enough to vitrify
the clay body).

or vermiculite, soaked in salt water. For more information about the range of colors that are possible with oxide colorants, see page 119 in the section on Glazes, Slips, and Colorants.

It's best to use an open clay body for the low-fire salt process. A raku clay body works well, or you can use any clay body that contains a high percentage of grog or sand, as long as it doesn't lose the *plasticity*, or workability, of the clay. Tighter clay bodies can be used, but you may have a higher percentage of cracking. Pieces must first be bisque fired to avoid firing breakage.

Modifying the Raku Kiln's Firing Chamber

Build a circular enclosure of firebrick, turning the bricks on end and stacking them so the wall will be higher than the ware (see figure 5, page 51). Make one or more small openings at the bottom of the firebrick wall to allow heat to enter the enclosure.

How to Fire

You can use any gas- or wood-fired fiber or brick kiln for the low-fire salt technique. Electric kilns, however, should never be used for this process, because the salt will corrode the elements in a short period of time. At the latter stage of the firing process, harmful hydrochloric acid vapors are emitted from the kiln. For this reason, the low-fire salt process should be done outdoors, away from a populated area.

1. Lay the brick on the shelf at the bottom of the kiln. Spread a layer of hardwood pieces around the brick, then sprinkle one-third of the salt over the wood (photo 71 on page 53).

2. Spray the ware with ferric chloride. Sprinkle copper carbonate on its shoulder, then lay a collar of wet clay, sprinkled with copper carbonate, over that (photos 72 and 73). Half-fill the cavity around the ware with sawdust. Add still more copper carbonate and another one-third of the salt (photos 74 and 75). Finish filling the cavity with straw and vermiculite.

3. Lay the two shelves across the top of the brick wall (photo 76) and top with the rest of the salt.

4. Fire the kiln to between cone 012 (1,616°F [880°C]) and cone 04 (1,958°F [1,070°C]). Remove the ware when the kiln has cooled (photo 77).

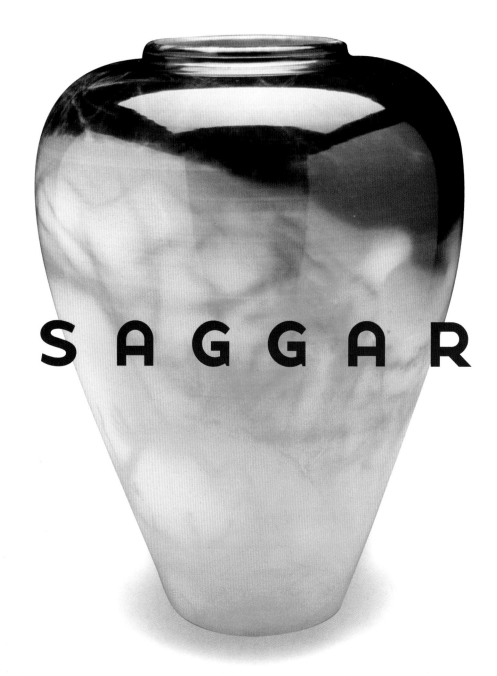

SAGGAR

SAGGAR FIRING

For those people who are looking for a luscious unglazed surface for their work, firing in a lidded metal or clay *saggar* (a reusable, heat-resistant container) offers spectacular results. Saggar firing was invented in China during the Sung Dynasty and is still being used today. Originally, the term (which may have come from the word "safe-guard") referred to a container made of fire clay. In the 19th and early 20th centuries, saggars in America and Europe were used to protect porcelain and stoneware from vapors, ash, or debris in a kiln. During that time large commercial ceramic factories had their own saggar-making departments. These saggars, made in many sizes and shapes, could last for 30 or 40 firings before the clay began to break down.

Today ceramic artists use the term saggar more loosely, to mean any container made of *refractory*, or heat-resistant, material that will hold clay objects during firing. A creative use of the saggar is to place combustible materials *inside* it that will carbonize, flash, or blush the surface of the ware for visually exciting surface effects. A variety of salts is used in atmospheric firings (such as saggar and pit firings) to achieve a marbled texture of warm earth tones. Each type of salt, whether Epsom salt, copper sulfate, baking soda, or table salt, will produce different shades of earth tones. For instance, Spanish moss, soaked in copper sulfate and dried, will leave a carbon image of the moss with an earth-toned halo created by the copper sulfate flashing onto the ware. Other materials soaked in salts, such as wood chips, hay, or vermiculite, will have similar effects. For more information about how oxides can be used to add color to clay and glazes, see the section on colorants (page 119).

James demonstrates several different surface treatments and saggar designs in this chapter. His favorite type of saggar is a metal one with a tight lid. For small work he uses inexpensive 5-gallon (19 L) popcorn cans, which may be found at garage sales. They'll last for approximately five firings. For larger work he employs a metal container made by a machine shop from $^1/_{16}$-inch (1.6 mm) black steel. Amazingly, it has lasted for three years without burning up. This metal saggar has a longer life than any of his clay saggars, but clay saggars can be made to custom-fit larger or unusually shaped pieces.

Saggars may be stacked on top of each other so that no shelves are needed inside the kiln. Never use a galvanized metal can, such as a metal trash can, as a saggar. The heat from the kiln will cause the galvanized metal to emit toxic zinc gas.

Rafael Molina-Rodriguez
Vasija, 1997
13 x 10 x 10 in
(33 x 25.4 x 25.4 cm); sprung arch
natural gas downdraft kiln; fired to
Δ 010 in clay saggar with sawdust,
salt-soaked hay, and sodium
chloride (salt)
Photo by artist

Terra sigillata with masked resist on bisque ware; toilet paper–wrapped in metal-can saggar firing by James C. Watkins.

Silver-Black Terra Sigillata with Masked Resist

Institutional-grade toilet paper (the hard stuff) doesn't seem a likely ingredient for creating a metallic black surface, does it? James has found that this inexpensive ingredient can produce a wonderfully rich and varied finish when it's used as a combustible material to saggar fire ware covered with terra sigillata. Attaining a completely carbonized surface can be an elusive goal, but even more elusive is the holy of holies: a silvery black surface.

How to Fire

Take care when you open the lid of any tightly fitted saggar. It should be cool to the touch, or an explosion could occur due to the sudden exposure of unburned materials to oxygen.

1. Draw designs on the bisque ware with a pencil (photo 1).

2. Mask the drawing with automobile masking tape (photo 2).

3. Use a brush or atomizer to paint the ware with a thin coat of terra sigillata (photo 3).

4. Use a soft cloth or chamois to buff the ware and bring out a shine on it (photo 4).

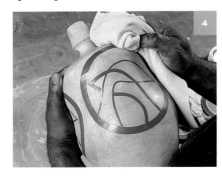

5. Remove the tape from the ware and wrap it to a thickness of 1 inch (2.5 cm) with toilet paper (photos 5 and 6).

Materials and Tools

Bisque ware

Pencil

Automobile masking tape

Hake brush or atomizer

Terra sigillata*

Soft cloth or chamois

Inexpensive toilet paper

Metal popcorn can with tight-fitting lid

Newspaper

Refer to page 39 for the recipe.

Ruth E. Allan
First Fruit, 2001
**9 x 14 in (23 x 36 cm); unglazed;
propane downdraft car kiln; fired to
Δ 03–04 in free-brick saggar lined
with chimney liner, with sawdust
and shavings**
Photo by Doug Yaple

6. Place wares on top of each other inside the saggar. Empty spaces may be filled with newspaper (photo 7).

7. Place the saggar inside the kiln and fire it to cone 012 (1,652°F [900°C]), as shown in photo 8. The deeply black surface (photo 9) has a heavy deposit of carbon on it because there wasn't enough oxygen to completely burn the combustible material inside the saggar.

Multicolored Surfaces

You can successfully obtain multiple colors by using either a lidded metal saggar or one made of clay. Whichever type you use, the saggar must have holes to control the oxygen flow into the saggar's interior. To get a variation of tone on the surface of the ware in each firing, increase the carbon absorption by plugging the holes with rolled-up, heat-resistant fiber blanket. The more holes you close, the darker the ware will be.

Electric kilns should never be used for this process because the salt will corrode the elements over a short period of time. When firing with salts and chemical metals, wear a respirator with filtration for fumes, organic vapors, and dust, because they release toxic chlorine and hydrochloric acid vapors as well as metallic fumes.

Chemical and natural materials fumed on bisque ware, saggar fired by James C. Watkins.

Materials and Tools

Bisque ware

Metal or clay saggar

Metal-cutting tool

Terra sigillata*

Hardwood sawdust

Small hardwood blocks

Kosher salt

Copper carbonate

Straw and vermiculite,
soaked in salt water
and dried

012–010 cones

Refer to page 39 for the recipe.

How to Fire

To avoid problems with cracking, use a bisque-fired and burnished white clay body, or apply terra sigillata to nonwhite bisque-fired ware.

1. Cut a series of holes, 1 inch (2.5 cm) in diameter and 6 inches (15.2 cm) apart, around the middle of the can (photo 10). Cut a 1- to 2-inch (2.5–5 cm) hole in the center of the lid.

2. Apply a thin layer of terra sigillata to the ware (photo 11).

3. Fill the saggar with combustibles. First, cover the bottom of the saggar with 6 inches (15.2 cm) of hardwood sawdust. The sawdust will create a deep black to dark gray color. Then place some wood blocks up to the halfway point around the piece.

4. Sprinkle kosher salt mixed with copper carbonate around the ware and on top of the dried materials (photo 12). Add more wood blocks (photo 13). Finish covering the ware with the dried, salt-laden straw, then vermiculite (photos 14 and 15). The smaller materials will settle between the spaces in the hardwood and create colors that range from light red to orange.

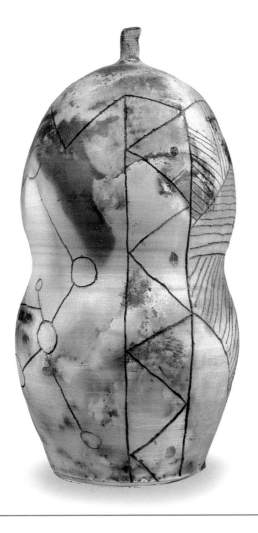

Stephen Carter
Untitled, n.d.
17 x 7 x 7 in (43 x 18 x 18 cm);
gas kiln; saggar-fired
Photo by artist

5. Cover the saggar with the lid and load it into the raku kiln (photo 16). Fire it to cone 012–010 (1,652–1,686°F [900–1,120°C]). Allow the saggar to cool to the touch before opening it (photo 17).

TIP

Many artists sprinkle or spray other chemicals around their work, such as potassium bichromate, iron chloride, or copper sulfate. Fine copper wire can also be wrapped around the ware to produce a distinctly colorful line.

Nearly any organic material is suitable for use as a reduction combustible to produce subtle earth tones. Some of these materials are seaweed, various fruit or vegetable peels, grass clippings, dried flowers, dried pet food, and horse and cow manure. Let your imagination run free.

Terra sigillata on bisque ware, fired in aluminum-foil saggar in downdraft stovepipe barrel by Don Ellis.

Aluminum Foil Saggar

The preparation for the aluminum foil saggar method is fun and simple, and work fired in this way has a colorful, mottled surface of reds, pinks, and browns. Any clay body can be used for this process. Lighter colored clay or porcelain bodies yield stronger and brighter colors, while darker bodies will have warm, muted earth tones. As you practice this technique you'll be better able to control the color patterns.

How to Fire

Electric kilns should never be used for this process because the salt will quickly corrode the elements.

1. Wearing rubber gloves, spray ferric chloride on the surface of your pot (photo 18). A light, even coat is all that's needed to create color during the firing.

2. Once you've covered the entire piece you can create accent areas on the work. Spray a concentrated area with the ferric chloride until the liquid sits on the surface rather than soaking into it (photo 19). While it's still wet, sprinkle some salt on the surface. The salt will create rust-colored spots wherever it directly touches the surface. Continue to spray the piece until it's completely covered (photo 20).

3. Tear off two sheets of foil large enough to cover the ware. Crumple the foil so that it has a very irregular surface. The purpose is to create small air pockets that will result in random patterns wherever the foil touches the piece. Spread the foil flat and sprinkle 2 tablespoons (30 g) of salt in the center area (photo 21).

4. Sprinkle 1 to 2 tablespoons (5–10 g) of the copper sulfate and follow that by adding a few clumps of the treated Spanish moss (photo 22).

Materials and Tools

Bisque ware

Rubber gloves

Ferric chloride (undiluted)

2-piece disposable spray gun with refillable container and propellant unit, for the ferric chloride

Table salt

Heavy-duty aluminum foil

Copper sulfate

Spoon

Spanish moss soaked in copper sulfate solution,* then dried

*2 tablespoons (5–10 g) copper sulfate in 8 ounces (.24 L) water

Katie Holland
I Think, Having Never Seen You, **2003**
42 x 36 x 36 in (1.05 x 1 x 1 m);
updraft gas kiln; fired in brick saggar
boxes; first firing to Δ 010 in sawdust,
salt-soaked shredded paper, Epsom
salts, and charcoal; second firing to
Δ 02 with sawdust, paper soaked in
baking soda, Epsom and other salts,
soda ash, and charcoal
Photo by artist

5. Place the ware in the center of the foil and put more moss on top. Bring the foil up around the ware's neck (photo 23). Crumple up more foil if needed to completely cover it. Roll the foil-covered piece so the loose materials are spread around a little more inside the saggar.

6. Now you're ready to load the raku kiln. You can tumble-stack foil saggars in the kiln until it's full (photo 24). Start the raku kiln and fire it to 1,166°F (630 °C). You'll notice at the end of the firing that some of the foil burned off (foil breaks down at 1,050°F [566°C]). This is normal; it means that the kiln reached the desired temperature.

7. When the raku kiln has cooled you can unload it. Remove the remaining foil and ash from the pot's surface (photo 25).

Iridescent Luster Fuming in a Clay Saggar

Make a clay saggar for a piece that won't fit into a metal saggar. The vessel shown here combines one of Biz Littell's formulas with a commercial metallic glaze.

Stannous chloride fuming on glazed ware by James C. Watkins.

Clay Body for a
Clay Saggar

41.8	Fire clay
20.8	Ball clay
20.8	Grog
8.3	Ground-up soft firebrick
8.3	Sawdust
100.0	Total

This is coarse clay, so throw it with gloves. Fire the saggar to the clay's maturity, cone 10 (2,377°F [1,303°C]), before you use it to fire pieces. (If the saggar is used before it has been vitrified it will absorb carbon and salts, which will increase the chance of early cracking.) Don't add sand as filler to the saggar clay formula, since the quartz inversion would cause the saggar to crack.

The 1-inch (2.5 cm) holes and plugs in James Watkins' clay saggar help him control the amount of oxygen that can enter it during the reduction phase.

Materials and Tools

Bisque-fired ware

Automobile masking tape

Brush

Duncan's SY 553 Antique Brass glaze

Wax resist

Biz's Black Underglaze #3*

Glaze spray apparatus

Playground sand

Clay saggar

Heavy-duty scissors

Fiber blanket

Tongs

Pyrometer

3 tablespoons (55 g) stannous chloride in a small plastic cup

See page 119 in the Glazes, Slips, and Colorants section.

How to Fume in a Clay Saggar

Review the cautionary information about stannous chloride on page 47.

1. Apply a masking tape motif to the bisqued piece. For more information about masking, see page 57.

2. Brush the masked area with the glossy Antique Brass glaze. Apply wax resist over the glazed area, then remove the tape.

3. Spray two light, even coats of Biz's Black Underglaze #3 (see page 119) onto the ware.

4. Spread a shallow layer of sand in the bottom of the saggar to protect it against thermal shock. Cut two pieces of fiber blanket to the size of a firebrick, and place them opposite each other on the bed of sand.

5. Load the work into the kiln and fire it to cone 04. Let the kiln cool to 900°F (482°C), then use the tongs to move the work, and two of the hot bricks from the kiln's baffle, into the clay saggar. Place the bricks directly onto the fiber blanket rectangles (photo 26). The temperature is important, so check it with a pyrometer.

6. Sprinkle the stannous chloride onto the hot bricks (photo 27).

7. After 1 minute, briefly raise the saggar lid (photo 28), then replace it. Let the ware cool before removing it (photo 29).

Judith Day
Amazon II, **2003**
30 x 14 x 6 in (76 x 36 x 15 cm);
platinum luster–fumed Kosai ware
Photo by artist

PIT FIRING

Paul Wandless demonstrates pit firing, a process that lets him enjoy being out-doors, working with clay, and experimenting with different types of exciting finishes. The pit is simply a hole, dug in the ground, that's used as a firing chamber. The pit contains the heat so that the interior reaches temperatures high enough to create a variety of finishes, in a range of blacks and grays or col-orful blushes of pinks, reds, and peaches. A white or light clay body or porcelain make the colors from the flames and reduction more pronounced because of their greater contrast. Darker clay bodies and earthenware mute the colors and result in warm earth tones.

Early cultures discovered clay in the ground and probably first experienced its plasticity and firing qualities by accident. This may have happened by find-ing some burnt and hardened clay in a camp or cooking fire. The earliest firings were done in aboveground open fires or bonfires. In some regions of Africa, the clay pots and objects are stacked in an open area. A mound of brush, grass, and other indigenous combustibles are used to cover the ware, then burned to cre-ate wonderful gradients of blacks and grays on the surfaces. In Mexico there's a similar variation of firing, in which the burnished work is tumble-stacked on the ground over a bed of wood. The stacked mound of pots is covered with more wood, then coals are added to start a bonfire. More wood and kindling is added as needed throughout the firing to manage the temperature of the fire, which lasts about an hour. This hotter fire creates rich blacks and strong variations of gray. These simple types of firings are still used today for utilitarian and cere-monial purposes by many cultures around the world.

Rebecca Urlacher
Untitled, 2002
**20¹/₂ x 9 x 4 in (52 x 22.9 x 10.2 cm);
bisque ∆ 05 electric; pit fired with saw-dust, sticks, and yard debris reduction**
Photo by David Simone

**Pit firing by Ray Rogers,
Wiltshire, England**
Photo by David Jones, courtesy
of The Crowood Press, England

Preparing the Pit

The first step in pit firing is digging a hole. If you're digging in your backyard, first have the local utility company indicate where there may be underground telephone or power cables. This service is normally provided for free. Clear an area, roughly 6 feet (1.8 m) in diameter, of any combustible items such as paper, trash, or brush. The size and amount of the work that you plan to fire will determine the depth and width of your pit. For small work, start with a pit 24 inches (61 cm) deep and 24 inches (61 cm) across.

**Pit fired with sawdust
reduction by Paul Wandless**

How to Fire

Because of the fire and smoke that's created it's important to find an open space where it's permissible to light and burn a fire. Stay away from the heavy smoke. Also be aware of where the combustible materials are in relation to the pit firing. Never leave any open fire or pit firing unattended.

When you stack the wood and other materials, think about how the ware will settle as the fire burns. Avoid an arrangement wherein sections of burning wood might collapse suddenly and break the pots underneath them. The hot embers will slowly burn the sawdust. To be safe, you should let the pit cool overnight; this will also ensure that you obtain the maximum surface effects from the process.

1. Layer the combustible material into the pit. Make a 3-inch (7.6-cm) bed in the bottom of the pit with a mixture of sawdust, kindling, and newspaper (photo 1).

2. The type of work you're firing will determine whether you want to use the metal rack. The grate keeps the work from tumbling during the firing; that's especially good for fragile pieces. Place the grill directly on top of the materials in the bed of the pit (photo 2). This helps airflow under the work and provides a place for the embers to settle. Place the work on the grill (photo 3). If you prefer, you can tumble stack the work on the bed swell. Keep in mind that pieces that touch each other or the wall of the pit will receive little or no smoke. You can use this to your advantage to purposely create unsmoked areas.

3. Pack the pit evenly with alternating layers of straw, sawdust, and newspaper. Loosely arrange some straw and newspaper around the pieces, adding a 3-inch (7.6-cm) layer of fine sawdust (photo 4). For this first layer, be sure to use only fine sawdust so that it will catch fire more easily when the embers reach it. Add another layer of straw and newspaper, this time following it with a 3-inch (7.6-cm) layer of coarse sawdust. Repeat the layering with coarse sawdust (or a mixture of coarse and fine) until the work is completely covered to a depth 3 inches (7.6 cm) over the ware.

Materials and Tools

Bisque ware

Fine and coarse sawdust

Kindling

Shredded newspaper

Metal grate or grill rack (optional)

Straw

Split wood

Lighter fluid

4. Put a layer of newspaper on top (photo 5). On top of the newspaper make a mound of split wood mixed with kindling so it burns more evenly.

5. Spray lighter fluid on the woodpile and let it soak in for a few minutes (photo 6). When you've sufficiently soaked the wood, light it in several places around the edges and also in the middle. Sometimes under windy conditions the fire will go out and must be relit a few times. Use the dirt from digging the hole to make a ring around the perimeter of the pit. This helps create a barrier to keep the fire from spreading (photo 7). If the com-

bustible material burns too quickly you can continue to add materials to the top of the mound. The fire should burn for 45 to 60 minutes, but the embers will remain hot for several hours. The fire will reach temperatures between 1,000 and 1,350°F (538–732°C).

6. After about 30 minutes the wood will be mostly gray, with some lazy flames still present (photo 8). Sometime during the next 30 minutes the flames will die out completely, leaving the hot embers to continue to burn their way through the combustible materials to the bottom of the pit (photo 9). Toward the end of the firing process, it's an option to cover the pit with more sawdust to smother the fire. This will cut off the oxygen supply and create a strong reducing atmosphere inside the mound.

7. Even after sitting overnight there may still be some hot embers in the bottom of the pit. Hold your hand above the pit to see if there's still heat emanating from it. If it's completely cooled you can remove the work (photo 10).

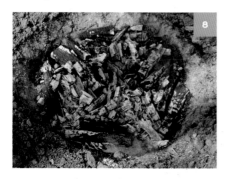

8. Douse the pit with water to put out any smoldering coals and embers.

Sumi Von Dassow
Pit-Fired Pot, 2003
8 x 10 x 10 in (20.3 x 25.4 x 25.4 cm);
pit with perforated pipe; sprayed with copper sulfate-salt solution; fired 6 hours with salt, banana peels, sulfates, Miracle Gro, hardwood scraps, and aspen logs
Photo by artist

Removal and Cleaning

Some of your work will need to be cleaned up a little. Cleaning is simple and fast and allows you to put sheen on the work. This will accentuate the marks of the flames and smoke. Depending on what combustibles were used, some surface attention may be needed. Simple household cleaning supplies will suffice. Paul recommends a soft cloth, a small stiff brush, a sponge, and paste wax (photo 11).

1. Use a stiff brush to remove any crusty residue and to get into tight cracks and textured areas (photo 12).

2. Wipe the surface clean with a damp sponge to get the rest of the soot and loose ash off the surface (photo 13). Let the work dry for about 10 minutes.

3. Apply the paste wax with the soft cloth and let it sit for 15 minutes (photo 14). Once the wax has dried, polish the surface (photo 15). This will darken the colors a little, revealing some of the more subtle colors, and it will also seal the surface, giving it a beautiful, rich appearance.

Sumi Von Dassow
Pit-Fired Jar, 2003
12 x 8 x 8 in (30.5 x 20.3 x 20.3 cm);
pit with perforated pipe; sprayed with
iron and copper sulfates-salt solution;
wrapped in newspaper with salt-
soaked pine needles; fired 6 hours
with salt, banana peels, sulfates,
Miracle Gro, hardwood scraps, and
aspen logs
Photo by artist

TIPS

The pit firing process continues to evolve as ceramists experiment with different materials, clay bodies, and approaches, each yielding different colors and effects. Here are a few ideas that you can experiment with, as you become more proficient with the process, to better suit your particular body of work.

To obtain more variations in color, apply and buff terra sigillata to bisque ware before firing it. Or, if you prefer, burnish green ware to give the surface an even smoother and shinier appearance. For a decorative layer of a different color you can

reapply terra sigillata after firing the first layer of it.

Washes made with colorants, such as black iron oxide, red iron oxide, and copper carbonate, can be applied to the bisque surface to create different color effects. (A wash is a mixture of water and an oxide or carbonate.) Dissolve 1 teaspoon (15 g) of the colorant in 8 ounces (.24 L) of water; you can modify this ratio to vary the concentration to your own preference. Refire the ware to cone 04 to create a base color on the surface before you proceed to pit fire the work.

Flashes (colored surface effects) can also be achieved by spreading dry oxides and carbonates, such as copper sulfate, rock salt, and baking powder, around and on the pieces as you're packing the pit. These chemicals will vaporize during the firing. Wrap copper wire or copper mesh around the pot to create interesting linear marks. Experiment and see what works best for you. Remember to always be careful handling chemicals. Keep them away from food, drink, children, and pets. Wear rubber gloves if spreading the chemicals by hand.

BARREL FIRING

Barrel firing is another outdoor firing technique that creates beautiful results and is enjoyable to do. As with pit firing, you can hang around the barrel and take pleasure from the fire and being outdoors—try it in the early evening hours, as the sun goes down.

Barrel firing doesn't have as long a history as pit firing, but it has been used for quite some time, and the move from an open fire to a contained one has some distinct advantages. A firing chamber reaches higher temperatures than does a pit, making it possible for added oxides, carbonates, and copper wire to produce stronger surface colors of red, ocher, and peach. Also, you can move a barrel from your storage area to a wind- and rain-protected one.

Linda Keleigh
Bottle, **2002**
**11 x 5 in (27.9 x 12.7 cm); burnished
terra sigillata; barrel-fired reduction
with wood, sawdust, pond grasses, and
copper carbonate**
Photo by artist

Burnished terra sigillata on green ware with chemical and natural-materials reduction by Linda Keleigh.

Terra Sigillata and Barrel Firing

Linda Keleigh shows how to burnish green ware, shares her terra sigillata recipe, and gives pointers on how to get interesting surface effects from a simple barrel firing. Her white terra sigillata provides a smooth, light-colored surface that contrasts well with the colors from the firing, making them more vivid. Burnishing gives your work a smooth surface that will become even more satiny when it's waxed after the firing. You could also use bisque porcelain or work coated with porcelain slip to achieve similar results. If you'd like a more muted finish on a nonwhite clay body, you can add colorants to the terra sigillata or eliminate it altogether. Keep in mind that each clay body will yield varied results.

Instructions

1. Mix together the first three ingredients of the recipe and set them aside.

2. Add the sodium silicate to the water and let it dissolve, then add the dry ingredients to this solution. Let it stand, undisturbed, for a minimum of 24 hours.

3. Once the solution settles into three layers, decant it, as described on page 39.

Preparing the Ware

You can choose to burnish your work at any point in the various stages of the clay's drying process, but it's advisable to match the burnishing tool to the degree of dryness of the piece. The drier the piece, the firmer the tool. With ware that is leatherhard or not quite bone dry, softer tools such as rubber ribs work best. Most artists experiment with various items, such as a smooth stone or a spoon.

1. Lightly sand a bone-dry piece with fine sandpaper to remove any surface imperfections (photo 1). Be careful not to press too hard or you'll break the piece.

2. Once you've sanded the surface, liberally apply baby oil to it and work it in with your hands (photos 2 and 3). Be sure to cover the entire surface for even results and allow the oil to soak in for a few minutes.

3. Wipe the piece lightly with a water-dampened paper towel (photo 4), being careful not to soften the clay too much. A too-wet surface may soften the clay, which might lead to distortion or breakage of the piece.

RECIPE

Terra Sigillata #2 for Green Ware

8½ cups (1,120.6 g) ball clay
12 cups (316 g) EPK
¼ cup (48.5 g) bentonite
2 teaspoons (7.5 g) sodium silicate
14 cups (3.3 L) water

Materials and Tools

Bisque ware

Fine grit sandpaper

Baby oil

Paper towels

Cylindrical porcelain bead (from a ball mill)

Soft cloth

Terra sigillata

Wide bamboo or hake brush

Linda Keleigh
Orb, 2003
5¹/₂ x 10 in (14 x 25.4 cm); burnished
terra sigillata; barrel-fired reduction
with wood, sawdust, pond grasses,
and copper carbonate
Photo by artist

4. Use the bead or other burnishing tool to burnish the surface in one direction (photo 5). When you've burnished the entire surface, finish it by changing direction (photo 6), and repeat the burnishing. This will achieve the smoothest effect.

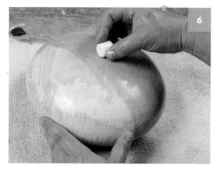

5. Apply a layer of terra sigillata over the entire surface (photo 7), then buff the pot with the soft cloth (photo 8).

6. Bisque fire the burnished green ware to cone 010, so that the piece will remain fairly porous. This allows for greater penetration and trapping of the carbon and vapors from the colorants into the ware's surface. The ware is ready to fire.

Preparing the Barrel

If you have several pieces you can tumble stack them in the barrel, making sure the larger ones are on the bottom and the smaller and lighter work is at the top (figure 7). This helps prevent breakage as the work settles during the firing. Using a half-barrel also helps you avoid the temptation to stack too many pieces into one firing. As the fuel consumes the oxygen, you're creating a reduction atmosphere that will deposit blacks and grays on the surface. As the fire burns down and the ashes fall away the atmosphere becomes reoxidized, which creates lighter color values, most notably in the copper range.

As an option for more color and surface decoration you can wrap your work with copper wire (photo 9) wherever you would like lines on the surface. Simply twist together the wire ends to keep them in place. The wire should be tight to the surface for any effects to take place.

Tumble-stacked barrel firing is simple and quick.

FIGURE 7

Linda fires two barrels at once, since it's just as easy as firing one.

Materials and Tools

55-gallon (209 L) metal barrel or oil drum, cut in half	Copper carbonate
Sawdust	Plastic cups
Straw	Paper towels
Red iron oxide	Split wood and kindling
Coarse salt	Lighter fluid
	Other dry natural combustible material

How to Fire

The amount of color achieved will depend on weather conditions, the combination of chemicals used, the speed of the firing, and the heat of the fire. If you're not satisfied with the results, you have the option of refiring the work multiple times, until you get the surface you desire.

1. Layer the bottom of one barrel with sawdust and the other with straw. The sawdust bed will smolder longer and smoke the work a little heavier, resulting in darker surface coloration, than will the bed of straw.

2. Put small amounts of the colorants and salt in separate plastic cups. Sprinkle a small amount of the red iron oxide into the barrel, along with an equal amount of the coarse salt (photo 10). Red iron oxide typically produces shades of orange and salt usually yields yellows. You don't have to completely cover the combustible material; just disperse it evenly over the area where you'll lay your work.

3. Place the work on the bed in any arrangement you like. Be sure to place them so the flames, smoke, and colorants can affect as much surface as possible (photo 11). Remember that there will be some settling and movement in the firing as material burns away. Arrange the work with heavier pieces at the bottom and lighter ones on top to minimize potential damage. Alternatively, you may wish to have the pieces touching in order to leave resist markings. The smoke will be blocked where the pieces touch each other or the side of the barrel, leaving lighter or even white areas on the surface. In the left-hand barrel, Linda uses one vessel as a minisaggar (filled with straw) to hold another piece; on the right, a paper towel drapes an orb.

4. Lightly sprinkle copper carbonate on top of and around the pieces (photo 12 on page 83). Copper carbonate is likely to produce shades of pinks to dark burgundy, depending on the amount you use.

Linda Keleigh
Platter, 2002
2 x 15 in (5 x 38.1 cm); burnished
terra sigillata; barrel-fired reduction with wood, sawdust, pond
grasses, and copper carbonate
Photo by artist

5. Add more straw (photo 13), until the work is completely covered. Make sure that straw also fills any open spaces between the work, although you don't need to pack or push it in tightly. The straw will make a good deal of smoke during the firing, creating lovely grays and blacks; you may also see a pattern of straw markings. Sprinkle more salt and red oxide on top of the straw (photo 14).

Use a 10-gallon (38 L) metal can for smaller work; the length of the burning period will be lessened proportionally.

Experiment with other combustibles, such as nutshells, dried banana peels, or seaweed, both below and above your pieces, to see what type of markings and colors each leaves behind. Create your own combination of combustibles for your own unique results. Soak and dry materials that are rich in organic elements, such as Spanish moss, in salt water and use them in conjunction with or in place of the salt. For more information about colorants, see page 119 in the Glazes, Slips, and Colorants section.

Make sure the combustibles are well dried before using. Wet or moist materials don't burn very well and will smoke very heavily, choking out the fire.

Try small amounts of different oxides or carbonates for various coloration effects. Use rubber gloves when appropriate to protect your skin.

6. Mound the wood, mixing in different sizes randomly with more of the kindling on top (photo 15). For safety's sake, don't stack the wood at the outermost edges of the barrel any higher than its top edge. To ensure a good start, add lighter fluid to the wood and let it soak in for a few minutes.

7. Now you're ready to light the barrel. If it's a little windy you may need to relight the fire a few times till it catches. There will be tall flames during the beginning of the burning. These flames will lower as the wood burns away, turns to hot embers, and finally begins to expose the work, giving you the first peak at finishes. The heavy burning of flames will die out in about 30 to 45 minutes. The other combustibles will continue to burn for 4 to 6 hours.

8. Once all the material has burned away and the barrel is cool you can unload your work (photo 16). Clean off the residue with soap and water on a sponge. For tough residue, use a scouring pad gently on the spot. If you're rough on it, you might scrape off the terra sigillata, leaving unsightly marks behind. Wax the piece, as described on page 74.

Downdraft Stovepipe Barrel Kiln

For all kiln designs, there is an alternative or modified version of the original, and the barrel kiln is no exception to this rule. You can modify a 55-gallon (206 L) barrel or oil drum with a stovepipe.

This type of kiln design is called a *downdraft* because it pulls oxygen strongly into the firing chamber, increasing the airflow to the fire and making the firing chamber even hotter (see figure 7). The downdraft kiln was developed in Europe sometime after 1800, and the design soon traveled to Japan, where it continued to evolve. These kilns are con-stantly being modified by ceramists the world over. The true downdraft kiln has a chimney stack three times the height of the firing chamber (plus added height for the horizontal measurement); nevertheless, Randy Brodnax's roomy barrel design achieves quick, even heat throughout the chamber.

For the inaugural firing, we used foil saggars. Randy recommends copper sulfate for deep reds and pinks, Spanish iron for oxblood, and burgundy and yellow ochers for medium reds. A few teaspoons of each will suffice, but you can experiment with other amounts to suit your visual needs. You can also sprinkle in colorants while you're loading the kiln, as demonstrated in the section on basic barrel firing (pages 82–83). The colors and variety of surface markings will vary from piece to piece, depending on where and how it was stacked for the firing. If you don't like the results you can always refire your work.

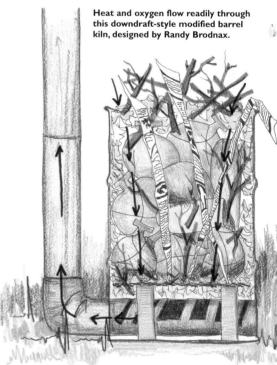

Heat and oxygen flow readily through this downdraft-style modified barrel kiln, designed by Randy Brodnax.

FIGURE 7

Materials and Tools

1 stovepipe elbow joint

Permanent marker

Paper

Scissors

55-gallon (209 L) metal barrel or oil drum with lid

Electric drill and ¼-inch (3 mm) drill bit for metal

Large flathead screwdriver

Hammer

6 straight stovepipe sections

Tin snips

Side grinder, with disk for cutting metal

1 soft firebrick

24 inches (.6 m) stovepipe wire

Wire cutters

24 x 8-inch (.6 m x 20.3 cm) piece of expanded metal

4 hard firebricks

Round metal grill rack

Building the Kiln

1. Trace the collar end of the elbow joint onto a piece of paper, then cut out the shape. Each section of the stovepipe has a narrow sleeve end and a wider collar end, so be sure to trace the correct one.

2. Use the paper shape to trace the cut line for the hole onto the side of the barrel, 1 inch (2.5 cm) up from the bottom edge; avoid the seam. Lay the barrel on its side and straddle it so it will be steady, then drill holes in the barrel, ¼ inch (3 mm) apart, along the line you drew (photo 17).

3. Place the head of the screwdriver at an angle, facing away from you, and punch out the metal between the drilled holes by driving the screwdriver through it with the hammer (photo 18).

4. Choose one stovepipe section to be used for the bottom of the barrel. If the pipe is too long, use tin snips to trim off the excess from the collar end. Starting 2 inches (5.1 cm) from one end, use the side grinder to cut a series of slots, 2 inches (5.1 cm) apart, along one-quarter of the pipe's circumference (photo 19). Stop 2 inches (5.1 cm) from the other end.

5. Assemble the stovepipe parts. Place the slotted section of pipe into the bottom of the barrel, making sure the slots are facing up and the sleeve end points to the hole in the barrel. Position the collar end of the elbow into the hole so that it juts into the barrel a short way (photos 20 and 21), fitting onto the sleeve end of the slotted pipe.

6. Stand the barrel upright to build the chimney. Connect two straight sections of stovepipe to the elbow joint. Cut a piece of soft brick to the size of the space between the barrel and pipe. Set the brick in place between the side of the barrel and the stovepipe, and secure them to the barrel by wrapping wire around them several times. Crisscross the wires for extra strength, then twist and cut the ends (photo 22).

7. To finish the chimney, fit together the remaining three straight sections of stovepipe, then add them to the top of the others already in place.

8. Bend the piece of expanded metal so it lies over the slotted stovepipe. This protects the slots from getting clogged with debris during the firing. Place the four hard bricks, standing on end, on either side of the slotted stovepipe (photo 23).

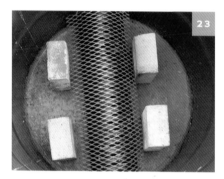

9. Lay the metal grill rack on top of the firebricks (photo 24). This shelf keeps the work from falling into the spaces on either side of the pipe.

Firing Materials

Wood shavings*

Small kindling

Newspaper

3 or 4 pieces of split wood

Lighter fluid

Kiln shelf shards, $3/4$ or 1 inches (1.9 or 2.5 cm) thick

Sold as pet bedding in pet stores sold, or substitute sawdust.

How to Fire

The size of the wood shavings and sawdust affects the speed of the burning process: the larger the particle size the faster it will burn.

1. Fill the bottom of the barrel with wood shavings, until it just covers the top of the grill rack (photo 25).

2. Tumble stack the work into the barrel. As you add ware, continue to add wood shavings and small kindling around it. Roll together several pages of newspaper into tubes. Place these lengthwise between the pieces (photo 26). This helps to keep the burn moving downward during the firing. After all the work is in, add enough wood shavings and small kindling to cover it with a 3-inch (7.6 cm) layer, with smaller bits of wood near the top (photo 27).

3. Soak three or four pieces of split wood with lighter fluid and place them on top of the stack in the center of the barrel (photo 28). Light the wood, then light any newspaper that is visible. After about 20 minutes the fire will burn down to short flames that dance on the surface of the sawdust. The burned wood will have formed into glowing embers that are starting to burn their way down through the sawdust pack.

4. Place three kiln shards, equally spaced apart, on the edge of the barrel (photos 29 and 30), then place the barrel lid atop them. Air will be drawn in through the space under the lid and pulled downward through the barrel. This draft of air is then pulled into the slotted stovepipe on the bottom, rising through the chimney and exiting as smoke. The process of the embers burning through and consuming the sawdust can take up to 10 hours. You won't see smoke out of the chimney right away. It can take from 30 minutes to 3 hours to create a strong downdraft. Be patient if it doesn't happen right away. Weather conditions—especially windy days—and how tightly the barrel is packed will affect the kiln's efficiency and burning speed.

5. Once all the combustibles have been consumed and the chimney stops smoking, let the barrel cool down. Randy recommends that you cool it overnight, or at least for a few hours. Removing the lid speeds up the cooling process. All the work will be exposed in the bottom of the barrel (photo 31). Once the work has cooled it can be removed and cleaned up.

6. To clean the work, enrich some of the colors, and bring out subtle markings, follow the same procedure as described for pit firing (page 74).

TIPS

You can control how quickly the downdraft effect starts. After you light the barrel, remove the chimney (the top three stovepipe sections). Pour a dozen red-hot charcoal briquettes into the pipe, then replace the chimney.

this page:

top:
Jan Lee
"Naked Raku" Form #2, 2003
8 x 6^1/$_2$ x 6^1/$_2$ in (20 x 17 x 17 cm);
**terra sigillata; bisque △ 010; fiber raku
tophat kiln; slip resist ("naked raku")
method fired to △ 014–016;
sawdust reduction**
Photo by Tim Barnwell

Jan pulls her "naked raku" piece when the
glaze first starts to mature (the cone
numbers are only a general guide), as it
takes on a pebbly look. Her "Wally's Slip"
and "Glaze Layer" formulas are in Glazes,
Slips and Colorants, on page 119, where
you'll also find a photo of the fired, broken
slip layer still adhered to the piece.

bottom:
Matt Wilt
Implements, 2001
**9 x 24 x 18 in (23 x 61 x 46 cm);
stoneware; gas kiln; fired to △ 8 in
reduction; cooled in reduction
atmosphere**
Photo by John Carlano

opposite page:

top left:
Lisa Maher
McKenna's Boot, 2001
**10 x 7 x 13 in (25 x 18 x 33 cm); fired
to △ 06 electric kiln in saggar with
seaweed and copper carbonate**
Photo by artist

top right:
Pat Sowell
Untitled, 1998
**8 x 8 in (20.3 x 20.3 cm);
bisque △ 05; reduction fired in brick
box packed with sawdust and hay,
with wood on top**
Photo by Butch Lieber

bottom left:
Terry Hagiwara
B & W Quilt, 2003
**11 x 8 x 8 in (28 x 20 x 20 cm);
white crackle glaze; gas raku kiln;
smoke fired in metal can**
Photo by Jack Zilker

bottom right:
James C. Watkins
*Double-Walled Platter
(from the Playa series),* 2000
**23 in diameter (58. 4 cm); glaze fired
to △ 04; terra sigillata over masked
design; buffed; fired to △ 012; crimped
newspaper reduction**
Photo by Hershel Womack

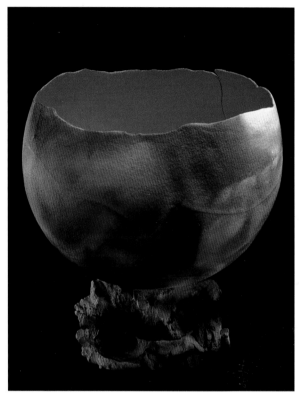

opposite page:

top left:
Reg Brown
Piestewa, Naked Raku, 2002
15 x 14 x 14 in (38 x 36 x 36 cm);
burnished stoneware; propane oil drum
fiber raku kiln; fired to Δ 06 with slip
resist ("naked raku") method and
newspaper reduction; water-shocked
cooling
Photo by Tommy Elder

The term "naked raku" was coined by
Charles and Linda Riggs of North Carolina.
It describes the glaze-resist process which
Reg used for this piece. Reg used Ramon's
Naked Raku Slip and Ramon's Transparent
Retaining Glaze formulas (see Glazes, Slips,
and Colorants, on page 119).

bottom left:
Linda Ganstrom
Seed Sisters, 2003
13 x 11 x 7 in (33 x 28 x 18 cm);
Δ 07 electric, cooled to 1,200°F (649°C);
air-cooled until crackled, then
newspaper reduction in metal can
Photo by Sheldon Ganstrom

bottom right:
Pat Sowell
Untitled, 1998
7¹/₂ x 8 in (19 x 20.3 cm); bisque Δ 05;
reduction fired in brick box packed with
sawdust and hay, with wood on top
Photo by Butch Lieber

this page:

top:
Beth Thomas
Seven Sisters Ewer, 1997
16 x 5¹/₂ x 5¹/₂ in (40.6 x 14 x 14 cm);
burnished terra sigillata; four-burner
natural gas updraft kiln; fired 12 hours
to Δ 010 in clay saggar with salt
water–soaked Johnson grasses and 22-
gauge copper wire
Photo by Tracy Hicks

bottom:
Marcia Selsor
Pryor Mountains Mustangs from Above,
1996
22 x 38 x 1 in (56 x 96.5 x 2.5 cm);
fiber kiln; fired to 1,850°F (1,010°C)
in straw reduction
Photo by artist

Marcia marks a clay slab with a drawing pencil,
masks it with latex resist, then sprays a
copper matte glaze onto it. After removing the
latex, she applies a thin line of copper luster
glaze around the edge of the drawing with a
hypodermic needle inserted into a modified
ear syringe. Then she fires the pieces standing
on edge. Her Copper Matte and Copper
Luster Glazes are on page 118 in Glazes, Slips,
and Colorants.

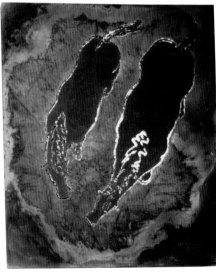

this page:

top:
Juan Granados
Morning Flight, 2003
11 1/4 x 5 3/4 x 4 3/4 in
(28.6 x 14.6 x 12.1 cm);
raku fired to Δ 04;
image/photo transfer
Photo by Jon Q. Thompson

bottom left:
Linda Ganstrom
Expectations, 2003
23 x 10 x 10 in (58 x 25 x 25 cm);
underglaze, crackle glaze, and gold
luster; Δ 07 electric, cooled to 1,200°F
(649°C); newspaper reduction inside
metal can
Photo by Sheldon Ganstrom

bottom right:
Paul Andrew Wandless
Simple Pair, 2003
21 x 8 x 7 in
(53.4 x 20.3 x 17.8 cm);
pit-fired with sawdust reduction
Photo by artist

opposite page:

top:
Tom Bartel
Dormant Head, 2002
14 x 10 x 10 in
(35.6 x 25.4 x 25.4 cm);
multi-fired; terra sigillata and
vitreous engobes fired to Δ 02;
black copper oxide fired to Δ 02
Photo by artist

bottom:
Gerard Ferrari
Inch of Soul, 2001
22 x 20 x 10 in
(56 x 50.8 x 25.4 cm);
electric kiln; fired in firebrick
saggar to Δ 04
Photo by Larry Dean

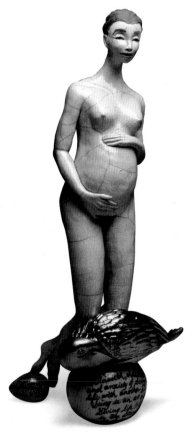

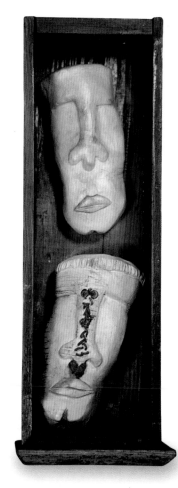

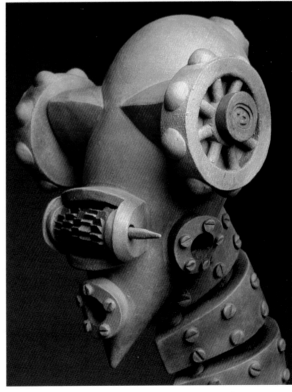

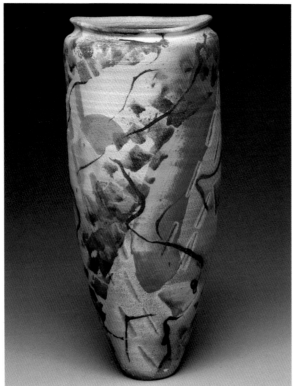

top:
Linda Ganstrom
Love to Play, 2003
20 x 6 x 6 in (51 x 15 x 15 cm) velvet underglazes, clear raku glaze, and gold luster; Δ 07 electric, cooled to 1,200°F (649°C); newspaper reduction inside two nested, lidded metal cans
Photo by Sheldon Ganstrom

bottom:
Sheldon Ganstrom
Nighthawk Vessel, 2002
36 x 16 x 14 in (91 x 41 x 36 cm); Δ 07 electric, then cool to 1,300 to 1,500°F (704–816°C); newspaper reduction inside nested, lidded containers
Photo by artist

opposite page:

top left:
Patrick Crabb
Shard plate series, 2003
21 x 17 x 3 in (53 x 43 x 8 cm); Δ 06 electric; gas raku kiln; reduction
Photo by artist

top right:
Charles and Linda Riggs
Lidded Saggar Jar, 2000
12 x 6¹/₂ in (31 x 17 cm); polished white terra sigillata; raku fired in clay saggar with sawdust, copper carbonate, salt, and steel wool reduction
Photo by J. D. Riggs

bottom left:
Charles and Linda Riggs
Large Altered Orb, 2002
11 x 11 in (28 x 28 cm); white stoneware; polished white terra sigillata; raku fired to 1,700°F (927°C) in clay saggar with sawdust, copper carbonate, copper scrub pads, salt, and steel wool reduction
Photo by Charles Riggs

Charles and Linda spray their stoneware with three coats of terra sigillata, buff it with a soft cloth or pantyhose, then bisque-fire to cone 08

bottom right:
James C. Watkins
Sleeping Posture, 1995
20 x 23 in (50.8 x 58.4 cm); buffed terra sigillata; fired to Δ 04; sawdust reduction
Photo by Mark Mamawal

opposite page:

top left:
James C. Watkins
Bi-Rhythms, 2001
6 x 12 in (15.2 x 30.5 cm); sprayed terra
sigillata; fired to ∆ 04; sawdust reduction
Photo by Hershel Womack

top right:
Maria Spies
Amphora with 3 Handles, 2001
20 x 8 x 8 in (51 x 20 x 20 cm);
terra sigillata; bisque ∆ 06; propane
clamshell raku kiln; custom-fit saggar
packed with fine sawdust, salt-soaked
hay, and copper carbonate and slow
fired to 1,550°F (843°C)
Photo by artist

bottom left:
Malcolm Smith
Body Poem I, 2000–2001
25 x 10 x 10 in (64 x 25 x 25 cm);
red terra sigillata; free-stacked coffin-
style pit kiln; fired on 6-inch (15.2 cm)
sawdust bed and packed with scrap
copper, small bisqued cups of various
sulfates and borax, brine-soaked
straw, additional sawdust, and kindling;
slow cooled
Photo by artist

bottom right:
Paul McCoy
Exquisite Agony, 2001
14¹/₂ x 9 x 9 in (37 x 23 x 23 cm);
terra sigillata (top) and velvet
underglaze (bottom); gas updraft kiln;
fired in airtight saggar to ∆ 06 in toilet
paper reduction; sandblasted
Photo by artist

this page:

top:
Bryan Hiveley
Grey Hook Teapot, 2003
16 x 14 x 6 in (41 x 36 x 15 cm);
bisque ∆ 04 ; fired to ∆ 06 reduction
in paper
Photo by artist

bottom:
Jane Perryman
Burnished Vessels, 2003
11 x 9 x 9 in (27.9 x 22.9 x 22.9 cm);
bisque-fired to 1,832°F (1,000°C); gas
kiln; saggar-fired to 1,472°F (800°C)
with sawdust
Photo by Graham Murrell

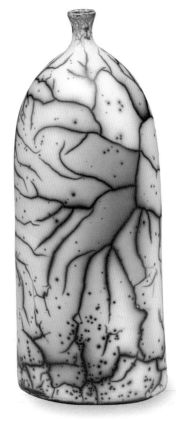

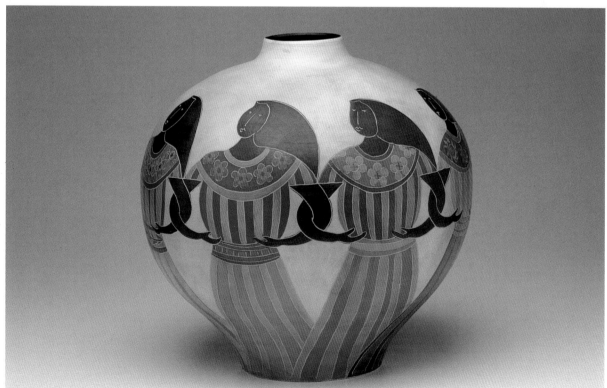

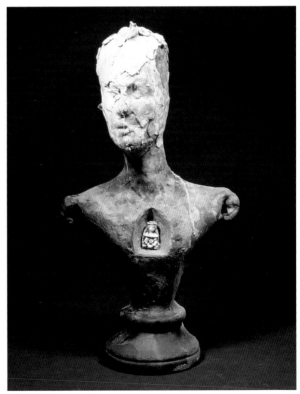

opposite page:

top left:
Virginia Mitford-Taylor
Saggar Vase, 2003
12 x 7¹/₂ in (30.5 x 19 cm); pit-fired in tin
saggar with seaweed, wood chips, copper
wire, and copper carbonate
Photo by Pat Crabb

top right:
Judith Motzkin
Spirit Keeper, 2000
15 x 11 x 11 in (38 x 28 x 28 cm);
custom-fit clay saggar; electric kiln
converted to downdraft propane; fired
with straw or hay soaked in metallic
salts and oxides
Photo by Dean Powell

bottom left:
Ruth E. Allan
Sunrise #17, 1998
16 x 12¹/₂ in (40.6 x 31.8 cm); unglazed;
propane downdraft car kiln; fired to
Δ 03–04 in free-brick saggar with salt,
iron filings, iron and copper wires, and
masking tape
Photo by artist

bottom right:
Cara Moczygemba
Escape, 1999
24 x 13 x 10 in (61 x 33 x 25 cm);
pit-fired with copper fuming slip
and seaweed
Photo by artist

this page:

top:
Biz Littell
Warrior, 2000
30 x 20 x 10 in (76 x 51 x 25 cm);
gold-fumed Kosai ware
Photo by artist

bottom:
Don Ellis
Copper Matte Luster Vase, 2002
20 x 22 x 22 in (50.8 x 56 x 56 cm);
91% alcohol reduction in Pyrex chamber
Photo by artist

this page:

top:
Judith Motzkin
A Life of the Heart, 2001
14 x 15 x 4 in (36 x 38 x 10 cm);
fresco on plaster set with sawdust-
fired clay insets; electric kiln
converted to downdraft propane;
fired with straw or hay soaked in
metallic salts and oxides
Photo by Susan Byrne

bottom:
Gary Greenberg
*Installationette (circus arachas
hypogaea),* 2001–2003
78 x 16 x 102 in (198 x 41 x 259 cm);
faux-foil firing method; borax and
water glaze; bisque Δ 05; gas
updraft kiln; fired in foil wrapping
to Δ 010–012
Photo by artist

opposite page:

top left:
Sharif Bey
Assimilation? Destruction, n.d.
2 ft. high x 6 ft. diameter
(61 x 183 cm); earthenware; updraft
Alphine kiln; tumble stacked
Photo by Stephanie Schofield

top right:
Steven Branfman
Vessel, 1999
14 x 9¹/₂ x 9¹/₂ in (36 x 24 x 24 cm);
colored-glass inlay and clear raku
glaze; reduction in coarse sawdust
Photo by artist

bottom left:
Magdalene Odundo
Untitled, 1987
12³/₄ x 8 in (32 x 20 cm);
gas kiln; oxidized for red terra cotta,
carbonized for black
Photo by Johnathan Lynch

bottom right:
Rolando Shaw
Footed Form #2, 2003
7 x 4 x 5¹/₂ in (18 x 10 x 14 cm);
resist slip method; three-burner raku
kiln; shredded newspaper reduction
Photo by Harrison Evans

opposite page:

top left:
Avner Singer and No'a Ben Shalom
Untitled, 2002
32 x 156 x 1¹/₆ in (80 x 390 x 3 cm);
terra sigillata on heavily grogged clay;
black engobe silkscreen prints from
photographs; fired to 1,742°F (950°C);
aboveground pit, fired with wood slats
and sawdust, copper carbonate, and
table salt added to embers
Photo by Ran Erde

top right:
Nancy Farrell
Woman, 2001
35 x 13 x 13 in (89 x 33 x 33 cm);
sawdust and salt reduction
Photo by artist

bottom left:
Pat Sowell
Untitled, 1998
8 x 10 in (20.3 x 25.4 cm);
bisque Δ 05; reduction fired
in brick box packed with sawdust
and hay, with wood on top
Photo by Butch Lieber

bottom right:
Winnie Owens-Hart
Three Women, 1997
18.1 x 17¹/₂ in (46 x 44.5 cm);
earth trench; 24-hour firing in
sawdust and shredded paper; firing
time extended with damp newspaper
Photo by Jarvis Grant

this page:

top:
Susan Worley
Space Odyssey, 2003
5¹/₂ x 6¹/₂ in (14 x 17 cm);
copper-iron wash over white slip;
fired in raku kiln; metal can smoking
with brief reoxidation
Photo by Lynn Hunton

bottom:
Eduardo Lazo
Aurora Borealis, 2002
10 x 12 x 12 in (25 x 30 x 30 cm);
multifire glazes; postfiring
chemical fuming
Photo by Paul Titangos

this page:

top:
James C. Watkins
Double-Walled Bowl
(from the Guardian Series), 2003
**9 x 19 in (22.9 x 48.3 cm);
copper wash glaze; fired to 1,700°F
(927°C), cooled to 800°F (427°C);
stannous chloride fuming**
Photo by Hershel Womack

bottom:
Cindy Couling
Fish Tale, n.d.
**6 x 7 x ³/₄ in (15 x 18 x 2 cm);
printed linoleum block on B-Mix;
bisque Δ 06; copper and Kuroka Red
glazes; sawdust reduction**
Photo by Lynn Hunton

opposite page:

top left:
James C. Watkins
Bottle Form, 2001
**11 x 9 in (27.9 x 22.9 cm); glaze
fired to Δ 04; terra sigillata over
masked design; buffed; fired to Δ 012;
sawdust reduction**
Photo by Hershel Womack

top right:
Sumi von Dassow
Pit-Fired Vase, 2002
**9¹/₂ x 6¹/₂ x 6¹/₂ in
(24.1 x 16.5 x 16.5 cm);
burnished B-mix without terra
sigillata; pit fired with wood
shavings, salt, copper sulphate,
and Miracle-Gro**
Photo by artist

bottom left:
Ruth Allan
Celestial Presence, 2002
**15 x 13 in (38 x 22 cm); unglazed;
propane downdraft car kiln; fired to
Δ 03–04 in free-brick saggar with salt,
iron filings, soapflake chemicals, copper
and iron wires, and masking tape**
Photo by Doug Yaple

Ruth achieves a variety of marks with
different brands of masking tape, and also
places torn pieces of newsprint painted
with red iron oxide on her porcelain ware.
She surrounds the piece with many 2-inch
(5 cm) clay cups filled with salt, iron filings,
and low-flux minerals such as borax. The
fluxes and salt fume the filings, wire, and
oxide, and interact with the tape, creating
rich rust-colored areas on the clay.

bottom right:
Don Ellis
Copper Matte Luster Vase, 2002
**18 x 18 x 18 in
(45.7 x 45.7 x 45.7 cm);
91% alcohol reduction in
Pyrex chamber**
Photo by artist

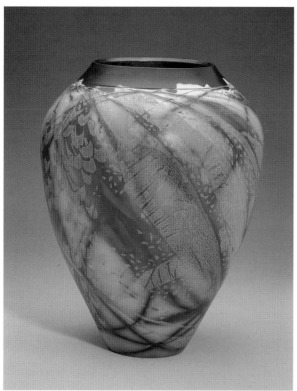

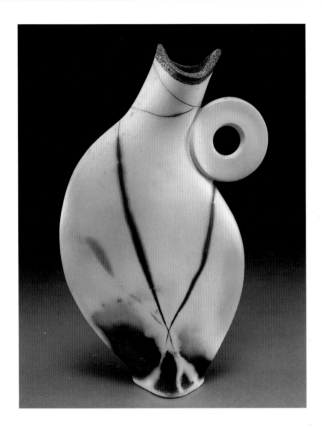

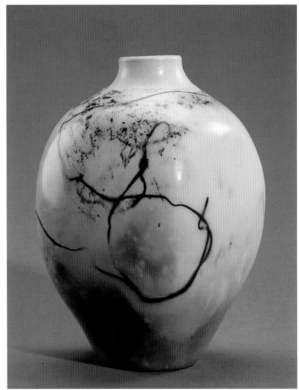

top left:
Shellie Hoffer
Dancing Pot, 2003
12 x 6.75 x 2 in (31 x 17 x 5 cm);
burnished porcelain; electric kiln; fired
to approximately Δ 010 in saggar with
seaweed, chickweed, copper wire,
steel wool, and salt
Photo by Courtney Frisse

Shellie uses copper wire to create black
lines, and picture-hanging wire for brown
ones. She sometimes soaks her reduction
materials in a solution of water and cobalt
sulfate, then dries them, firing the ware in a
tight clay saggar without any holes.

top right:
Judy Harper
"Squared-Off" Saggar-Fired Pot, 1999
6³/4 x 5³/4 x 5¹/4 in (17 x 13 x 13 cm);
agate-burnished porcelain; bisque Δ 06
electric; Δ 012 electric in clay saggar
with weeds, flowers, seaweed, steel
wool, copper, and sisal twine reduction
Photo by Roger Schreiber

bottom left:
James C. Watkins
Guardians, 1998
25 x 20 in (63.5 x 50.8 cm);
buffed terra sigillata; fired to Δ 04;
newspaper reduction
Photo by Mark Mamawal

bottom right:
David Jones
Dark Pool, 2002
11 x 10³/8 in (28 x 26 cm);
raku-fired double walled vessel
Photo by Rod Dorling, courtesy of David Jones and
The Crowood Press, Wiltshire, England

top:
David Joy
Untitled, 2002
19 x 26 x 26 in (48.3 x 66 x 66 cm);
custom updraft brick kiln built for
each piece; foil saggar-fired with
copper-tape masking, iron and copper
salts, paper, and hay
Photo by Bruce Fairfield

bottom:
Sumi von Dassow
Mystery of the Deep, 2003
9 x 9 x 9 in (22.9 x 22.9 x 22.9 cm);
pit fired with horse stall bedding,
wood shavings, coffee grounds,
salt, copper sulfate, seaweed,
and Miracle-Gro
Photo by artist

this page:

top left:
Virginia Mitford-Taylor
Saggar Pot, 2002
12 x 5¹/2 in (30.5 x 14 cm);
electric kiln to Δ 010; saggar-fired in
metal can with seaweed, wood chips,
copper wire, and copper carbonate
Photo by Pat Crabb

Virginia drilled ¹/4-inch (6 mm) holes, 3 or 4
inches (7.6–10.2 cm) apart, around the top
and bottom of her metal saggar.

top right:
Judy Harper
Sliced Sagger-Fired Pot, 2001
10¹/2 x 4¹/2 x 4¹/2 in (27 x 11 x 11 cm);
agate-burnished porcelain; bisque
Δ 06 electric; Δ 012 electric in
clay saggar with weeds, flowers,
seaweed, steel wool, copper, and
sisal twine reduction
Photo by Roger Schreiber

bottom:
Juan Granados
Replacement VI, 2003
8 x 10 x 3¹/2 in (20.3 x 25.4 x 8.9 cm);
raku fired to Δ 04; image/photo
transfer
Photo by Jon Q. Thompson

opposite page:

top left:
Terry Hagiwara
My Cubism, 2003
10¹/2 x 9 x 9 in (27 x 23 x 23 cm);
metallic red, alligator, and white
crackle glazes; gas raku kiln;
reduction in metal can
Photo by Jack Zilker

top right:
Magdalene Odundo
Untitled, 1988
15¹/2 x 9 1/8 in (39 x 23 cm);
gas kiln; oxidized for red terra cotta,
carbonized for black
Photo by Jonathan Lynch

bottom left:
James C. Watkins
Double-Walled Bowl
(from the Guardian Series), 2001
9 x 19 in (22.9 x 48.3 cm).;
terra sigillata sprayed over masked
design on glaze; fired to Δ 04;
sawdust reduction
Photo by Hershel Womack

bottom right:
Richard Burkett
Pressure Vessel: Clamped, 2003
20 x 18 x 18 in (50.8 x 45.7 x 45.7 cm);
stoneware with barley burnout;
sprayed terra sigillata and copper
carbonate mixture; saggar-fired in
seaweed, vermiculite, sawdust, and
rock salt, with copper wire
Photo by artist

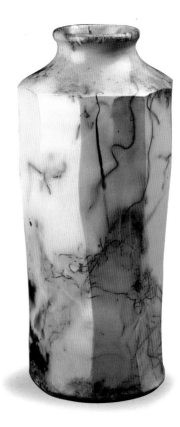

ACKNOWLEDGMENTS

To thank everyone who has given so much time, patience, and support for this project would probably fill another book. It takes a team effort from many different individuals to accomplish writing a book like this successfully. We are fortunate and

appreciative to have had dedicated, caring, and hardworking people around us to lend a hand along the way. We would like to thank Lark Books for the opportunity to write this book. We feel it is important to give something back to the field of ceramics, which has given so much to us over the years. We can't say enough about our editor, Suzanne Tourtillott, who has had unlimited patience and enthusiasm through this whole process. She kept us to our deadlines and answered at least 6,438 questions over the last year via phone, fax, and multiple e-mails. She quickly became our new best friend. Her guidance, support, and editorial expertise made this a much easier experience. A big and warm thank you also goes to Rob Pulleyn, who opened his beautiful home and studio to us for nearly a week for the photo shoot. Rob's generosity made everyone feel immediately at home, setting the tone for a dynamic, inspired, and creative atmosphere. After we were able to negotiate our way to the top of the mountain, we had an amazing stay. It is here where all the beautiful images were created with the guiding eye of art director Kathy Holmes and photographer Evan Bracken. They did a wonderful job capturing the many processes that were demonstrated and the beautiful surroundings in which they were performed.

We also want to thank Randy Brodnax, Don Ellis, and Linda Keleigh for participating and sharing their knowledge and techniques in this book. It is only with their willingness to give freely of their time, expertise, and enthusiasm that we could bring such a broad range of information to this project. They are not only wonderful artists, but also wonderful people whom we are happy to call good friends now.

James would like to thank his wife, Sara Waters, whose love and support are greatly appreciated, and his children, John Eric, Zachary James, and Tighe Marie, who are all a constant joy and inspiration. He is also grateful to his mother and father, who, in his formative years, made sure that he was never in want of art supplies. He also thanks his teachers throughout his life, from both academic environments and inter-

personal relationships, which includes students, colleagues, and friends.

Paul gives special thanks to his new wife and old friend, Jane, and their new son, Miles. Jane's daily support, encouragement, and belief in him made doing this much easier. He also thanks his brother, Danny, who has believed in his crazy dream to make art and has always supported it any way he could. He also thanks all his past professors and current colleagues, who all contributed to preparing him for this opportunity.

James C. Watkins
Paul Andrew Wandless

GLAZES, SLIPS, AND COLORANTS

All glazes should be tested before using them, since each will perform differently due to different conditions, quality of materials available, and the kiln used.

Raku Glazes

Black Gloss
Fire to Δ 06.

10.0	Borax
40.0	Gerstley borate
20.0	Soda ash
10.0	Nepheline syenite
20.0	Barnard clay
100.0	Total

+	4.0	Cobalt carbonate
+	2.0	Copper carbonate

Blue Crackle
Fire to Δ 06.

75.5	Gerstley borate
18.9	Cornwall Stone
5.6	Cobalt carbonate
100.0	Total

Blue Velvet
Fire to Δ 06.

30.0	Gerstley borate
10.0	Nepheline syenite
20.0	Aluminia oxide
20.0	Cobalt carbonate
20.0	Rutile
100.0	Total

Bob's Copper Red
Fire to Δ 06.

59.3	Gerstley borate
25.4	Feldspar G-200
8.5	Frit 3110
6.8	Black copper oxide
100.0	Total

Copper Blue
Fire to Δ 06.

66.6	Frit 3110
6.7	Gerstley borate
9.5	Silica (flint)
9.5	Soda ash
4.8	Kaolin (EPK)
2.9	Copper carbonate
100.0	Total

Copper Matte Glaze
Fire to 1,850°F (1,010°C). Marcia Selsor's *Pryor Mountains Mustangs from Above* (page 93) used this glaze and the Copper Luster Glaze #1.

66.6	Gerstley borate
16.7	Nepheline syenite
16.7	Bone ash
100.0	Total

+	7.0	Copper carbonate
+	3.0	Cobalt carbonate

Copper Luster Glaze #1
Fire to Δ 06.

75.0	Gerstley borate
25.0	Bone
100.0	Total

+	4.0	Copper carbonate
+	2.0	Cobalt oxide

Copper Luster Glaze #2
Fire to Δ 06.

80.0	Gerstley borate
20.0	Nepheline syenite
100.0	Total

+	1.1	Cobalt oxide
+	2.1	Copper oxide
+	7.8	Yellow ocher

Copper Penny
Fire to Δ 06.

80.0	Gerstley borate
20.0	Potash feldspar
100.0	Total

+	2.0	Copper carbonate
+	1.0	Cobalt carbonate
+	7.0	Yellow ocher

Ramon's Lithium Glaze
Fire to Δ 06. This versatile glaze produces varied colors within the firing temperature range: matte orange at 1,800°F (982°C) with partial postfire reduction; matte aquamarine at 1,820°F (993°C); and dark metallic brown at 1,850°F (1,010°C). Scrubbing the surface brings out copper highlights on pieces fired above 1,820°F (993°C). See Reg Brown's *Stolen Generations* (page 26).

28.5	Lithium carbonate
14.4	Kaolin (EPK)
57.1	Flint
100.0	Total

+	2.8	Bentonite
+	3.7	Copper carbonate

Ramon's Naked Raku Slip
Fire to Δ 06. Reg Brown's burnished vessel (page 92) used this slip under Ramon's Transparent Retaining Glaze, below.

60.0	China clay
40.0	Frit 3134
100.0	Total

Ramon's Transparent Retaining Glaze
Fire to Δ 06. Reg Brown's burnished vessel (page 92) used this glaze over Ramon's Naked Raku Slip, above.

15.0	China clay
85.0	Frit 3134
100.0	Total

Wally's Slip

Fire to △ 016–014. Mix to the consistency of milk. Jan Lee's *"Naked Raku" Form #2* (page 90) uses this slip under the Glaze Layer.

50.0	Highwater Raku Clay (dry)
30.0	EPK
20.0	Silica
100.0	Total

Glaze Layer

Fire to △ 016–014. Mix to the consistency of milk. Jan Lee's "Naked Raku" Form #2 (page 90) uses this glaze over Wally's Slip.

35.0	Gerstley borate
65.0	Frit 3110
100.0	Total

Fuming Glazes

Biz's Black Underglaze #1
Fire to △ 06–04 matte.

61.0	Ferro frit 3110
39.0	EPK
100.0	Total
+ 10.0	Black Mason Stain #6600
+ 2.0	Bentonite

Biz's Black Underglaze #3
Fire to △ 06–04 satin.

62.0	Ferro frit 3110
38.0	EPK
100.0	Total
+ 10.0	Black Mason Stain #6600
+ 2.0	Bentonite

Biz's Black Underglaze #4
Fire to △ 06–04 satin to gloss.

63.0	Ferro frit 3110
37.0	EPK
100.0	Total
+ 10.0	Black Mason Stain #6600
+ 2.0	Bentonite

Colorants

A glaze formula is typically given as a base formula which is modified by the addition of colorants. Use the recommended percentages to start testing the oxides listed here. Colorants react to glaze bases in different ways (hence the need for testing), and will react in the presence of other color opacifiers, such as tin, barium, or lithium. The color ranges described here are typical for alkaline glaze bases.

Copper carbonate

1.0 %	light turquoise
2– 3.0 %	turquoise to blue-green
5.0 % +	metallic green to black

Cobalt oxide

.25 %	light to medium blue
.50	strong blue
1.0 % +	blue-black

Chromium oxide

.5-3.0 %	a range of green

Iron chromate

2.0 %	grey-brown to black

Nickel oxide

1-2.0 %	muted browns

Manganese oxide

2-3.0 %	ranges from plum to purple-brown

Red iron oxide

1-3.0 %	ranges from ruddy brown to rust red

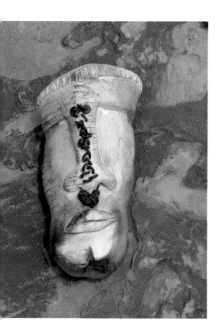

Pit-fired with sawdust reduction by Paul Andrew Wandless.

GLOSSARY

Alkaline glaze. Glazes in which sodium, potassium, lime, lithium, and magnesia are used as fluxes.

Baffle. A refractory wall in the kiln that redirects the flames away from the ware.

Banding wheel. A pedestal disk on bearings, rotated by hand, used to hold ware.

BTU. British thermal unit; measurement for a unit of heat used to express fuel ratings.

Bisque ware. Ware fired to an insoluble but porous state, which expels all the water from the clay body; usually done between cones 08 and 04.

Burner port. The opening in a kiln into which the burner is inserted.

Burner, venturi. A metal tube with a constricted throat that mixes propane gas with varying amounts of oxygen.

Burnishing. Rubbing or polishing leatherhard or dry clay with any firm, smooth tool; tightens the clay surface and compresses the clay particles.

Carbonaceous. Rich in carbon (see *reduction atmosphere*).

Ceramic insulation fiber blanket. A fibrous material that is both refractory and fire-resistant.

Colorant. A chemical substance which interacts with heat and other chemicals to create color effects on clay.

Combustibles. Materials such as sawdust, straw, and newspaper that are used as fuel during the firing process.

Cone, pyrometric. Small, elongated pyramid shapes of ceramic material that are designed to melt or bend at specific temperatures in a kiln. Each cone has a number indicating the temperature at which it will melt (see Orton cone chart, pages 122-123).

Downdraft kiln. A kiln where the chimney opening is at the bottom of the kiln, creating a strong downward flow of air in the firing chamber for the heat to escape. The heat initially moves up the firing chamber then is drawn back down through the ware.

Expanded metal. Sheet metal cut and expanded into a lattice form and used as lath for a raku kiln.

Firebrick, hard. A dense refractory brick, typically made of fireclay, that is able to withstand high temperatures and is heat-reflective.

Firebrick, soft. A porous, refractory brick that is heat-absorbent, also used as an insulator. It cuts easily and is used as furniture, such as baffles and shelf stilts, in the kiln.

Firing chamber. The area inside the kiln that holds ware.

Fuming. A technique by which materials are introduced into the firing chamber during the firing process, where they vaporize in the atmosphere and coat the ware's surfaces.

Glaze. A dense, vitreous, and glassy coating, created from a recipe of ceramic materials and chemicals, that has been melted onto a clay surface during the firing process.

Green ware. Unfired ware that is still in a malleable state, whether leatherhard or bone dry; the clay body still contains water.

Leatherhard. A stage in the drying process of green ware; the ware is dry enough so its surface is not sticky and it can support itself, yet it is still somewhat workable. Carving, burnishing, and joining of parts are commonly done at this stage.

Local reduction. A technique that creates carbon deposits on ware by placing combustibles directly on the hot surface.

Maturity. When referring to a clay body, the optimum temperature at which warping and brittleness are minimized and absorption is reasonably low. During firing the term is used to describe a glaze that is fully melted or has reached its desired visual effect; also referred to as *maturation point*.

MSDS. Material Safety Data Sheet; a document that contains information on the use, storage, handling, and emergency procedures related to a chemical product.

Nichrome refractory wire. Wire made from an alloy of nickel and chrome that is used in high-temperature conditions.

Oxide. An element that has combined with oxygen to form a new compound; used as a colorant in glaze and wash recipes or applied in its raw form directly to combustibles or ware.

Plasticity. The characteristic of a material to be worked or formed with ease, typically in the early stages of green ware when the clay is softest or most pliable.

Pyrometer. An instrument used to measure high temperatures inside a firing chamber.

Pyrometric cone. A pyramid-shaped piece of clay and flux, formulated to melt at specific temperatures inside the firing chamber.

Raku. A low-temperature ceramic firing technique for bisque ware, taken from the name of the ancient Japanese family that originated it. In Western practice a hot piece is pulled from the kiln at the glaze maturation point and immediately placed in combustible materials for smoke reduction.

Reduction atmosphere. Combustibles in contact with a hot piece create an atmosphere in which oxygen becomes a fuel and is then converted to carbon. This reduced, or polluted, atmosphere is referred to as a carbonaceous or carbon-rich atmosphere.

Refractory. Resistant to melting or fusion at very high temperatures.

Reoxidation. A process by which ware is reintroduced to oxygen, or an oxygen-rich atmosphere, after being in a carbonaceous or reduction atmosphere.

Saggar. A refractory container of clay or metal with a tight-fitting lid.

Terra sigillata. A very fine clay used for burnishing; often referred to as "terra sig" or "sig."

Thermal shock. The effects of the stress of expansion and contraction on clay due to sudden changes in temperature during the firing and cooling processes.

Tumble stack. Loading a kiln by placing wares directly on each other instead of using kiln shelves.

Vaporize. To cause a substance, such as a chemical, to evaporate by exposing it to intense heat or direct flame.

Vitreous. The state of a glaze or clay body that has been fired until it is dense, hard, and nonabsorbent.

Ware. A nonspecific term used to describe clay work.

Wash. A watery mixture of a colorant and water, used to stain ceramic ware in the green or bisque state.

Temperature Equivalents °F for Orton Pyrometric Cones

Cone	Self Supporting Cones 1¾" mounting height						Large Cones				Small 15/16" height	
	Regular			Iron Free			Regular		Iron Free		Regular	PCE
	27	108	270	27	108	270	108	270	108	270	540	270
Soft Series												
022	1049	1087	1094				N/A	N/A			1166	
021	1076	1112	1143				N/A	N/A			1189	
020	1125	1159	1180				N/A	N/A			1231	
019	1213	1252	1283				1249	1279			1333	
018	1267	1319	1353				1314	1350			1386	
017	1301	1360	1405				1357	1402			1443	
016	1368	1422	1465				1416	1461			1517	
015	1382	1456	1504				1450	1501			1549	
014	1395	1485	1540				1485	1537			1598	
013	1485	1539	1582				1539	1578			1616	
012	1549	1582	1620				1576	1616			1652	
011	1575	1607	1641				1603	1638			1679	
Low Temp Series												
010	1636	1657	1679	1600	1627	1639	1648	1675	1623	1636	1686	
09	1665	1688	1706	1650	1686	1702	1683	1702	1683	1699	1751	
08	1692	1728	1753	1695	1735	1755	1728	1749	1733	1751	1801	
07	1764	1789	1809	1747	1780	1800	1783	1805	1778	1796	1846	
06	1798	1828	1855	1776	1816	1828	1823	1852	1816	1825	1873	
05½	1839	1859	1877	1814	1854	1870	1854	1873	1852	1868	1909	
05	1870	1888	1911	1855	1899	1915	1886	1915	1890	1911	1944	
04	1915	1945	1971	1909	1942	1956	1940	1958	1940	1953	2008	
03	1960	1987	2019	1951	1990	1999	1987	2014	1989	1996	2068	
02	1972	2016	2052	1983	2021	2039	2014	2048	2016	2035	2098	
01	1999	2046	2080	2014	2053	2073	2043	2079	2052	2070	2152	
Intermediate Series												
1	2028	2079	2109	2046	2082	2098	2077	2109	2079	2095	2163	
2	2034	2088	2127				2088	2124			2174	
3	2039	2106	2138	2066	2109	2124	2106	2134	2104	2120	2185	
4	2086	2124	2161				2120	2158			2208	
5	2118	2167	2205				2163	2201			2230	
5½	2133	2197	2237				N/A	N/A			N/A	
6	2165	2232	2269				2228	2266			2291	
7	2194	2262	2295				2259	2291			2307	
8	2212	2280	2320				2277	2316			2372	
9	2235	2300	2336				2295	2332			2403	
10	2284	2345	2381				2340	2377			2426	
11	2322	2361	2399				2359	2394			2437	
12	2345	2383	2419				2379	2419			2471	2439

Temperatures shown are for specific mounted height above base. For Self-Supporting - 1¾". For Large - 2". For Small Cones - 15/16". For Large Cones mounted at 1¾" height, use Self-Supporting temperatures. The actual bending temperature depends on firing conditions. Charts provided with permission from The Edward Orton Jr. Ceramic Foundation.

Temperature Equivalents °C for Orton Pyrometric Cones

Cone	Self Supporting Cones 1¾" mounting height — Regular			Iron Free			Large Cones — Regular		Iron Free		Small 15/16" height — Regular	PCE
	15	60	150	15	60	150	60	150	60	150	300	150
Soft Series												
022	565	586	590				N/A	N/A			630	
021	580	600	617				N/A	N/A			643	
020	607	626	638				N/A	N/A			666	
019	656	678	695				676	693			723	
018	686	715	734				712	732			752	
017	705	738	763				736	761			784	
016	742	772	796				769	794			825	
015	750	791	818				788	816			843	
014	757	807	838				807	836			870	
013	807	837	861				837	859			880	
012	843	861	882				858	880			900	
011	857	875	894				873	892			915	
Low Temp Series												
010	891	903	915	871	886	893	898	913	884	891	919	
09	907	920	930	899	919	928	917	928	917	926	955	
08	922	942	956	924	946	957	942	954	945	955	983	
07	962	976	987	953	971	982	973	985	970	980	1008	
06	981	998	1013	969	991	998	995	1011	991	996	1023	
05½	1004	1015	1025	990	1012	1021	1012	1023	1011	1020	1043	
05	1021	1031	1044	1013	1037	1046	1030	1046	1032	1044	1062	
04	1046	1063	1077	1043	1061	1069	1060	1070	1060	1067	1098	
03	1071	1086	1104	1066	1088	1093	1086	1101	1087	1091	1131	
02	1078	1102	1122	1084	1105	1115	1101	1120	1102	1113	1148	
01	1093	1119	1138	1101	1123	1134	1117	1137	1122	1132	1178	
Intermediate Series												
1	1109	1137	1154	1119	1139	1148	1136	1154	1137	1146	1184	
2	1112	1142	1164				1142	1162			1190	
3	1115	1152	1170	1130	1154	1162	1152	1168	1151	1160	1196	
4	1141	1162	1183				1160	1181			1209	
5	1159	1186	1207				1184	1205			1221	
5½	1167	1203	1225				N/A	N/A			N/A	
6	1185	1222	1243				1220	1241			1255	
7	1201	1239	1257				1237	1255			1264	
8	1211	1249	1271				1247	1269			1300	
9	1224	1260	1280				1257	1278			1317	
10	1251	1285	1305				1282	1303			1330	
11	1272	1294	1315				1293	1312			1336	
12	1285	1306	1326				1304	1326			1355	1337

Temperatures shown are for specific mounted height above base. For Self-Supporting - 1¾". For Large - 2". For Small Cones - 15/16". For Large Cones mounted at 1¾" height, use Self-Supporting temperatures. The actual bending temperature depends on firing conditions. Charts provided with permission from The Edward Orton Jr. Ceramic Foundation.

ABOUT THE CONTRIBUTORS

Randy Brodnax, a lifelong potter and educator from Dallas, Texas, creates everything from functional dinnerware to large decorative vessels to clay sculpture. A Louisiana native, Randy has retained much of the Cajun joie de vivre of his childhood and has spent a career building bridges among clay artists of all levels of experience. In workshops Randy entertains the participants as he shares his knowledge with them, and helps individuals seeking a refined focus, new direction, or simply camaraderie among clay artists.

Don Ellis is from Cloudcroft, New Mexico, and has taught for many years at New Mexico State University at Alamogordo. He owns and operates Cloudcroft Pottery and does numerous workshops throughout the United States. Don holds a bachelor of science degree in education from McMurry University in Abilene, Texas, and a master's degree in ceramics from North Texas State University in Denton. He works almost exclusively in high-fire, functional stoneware.

Linda Keleigh is essentially self-taught and acknowledges the influences she acquired during various workshops and classes. Her formal education and early pro-

fessional career were focused in the financial arena, which was redirected after she discovered clay. In an attempt to provide a vessel of quiet beauty that is soothing to the senses, she has focused on employing primitive smoke-firing techniques to finely burnished clayware. Exhibitions of her work have included the LBI Foundation of the Arts Faculty Exhibition, Loveladies, New Jersey; Art Alliance of Monmouth County, Red Bank, New Jersey; Gallery of Brookdale's Center for Visual Arts, Lincroft, New Jersey; and Livingston Avenue Gallery, New Brunswick, New Jersey. She has gallery representation in numerous states, and her works are held in private collections internationally.

ABOUT THE AUTHORS

James C. Watkins is a ceramic artist who has been working with clay for over 30 years. His work is included in the White House Collection of American Crafts and the Shigaraki Institute of Ceramic Studies in Shigaraki, Japan. He is a full pro-

fessor and is the Assistant Dean of Undergraduate Studies in the College of Architecture at Texas Tech University in Lubbock. He is the recipient of the Texas Tech University President's Excellence in Teaching Award. He received a B.F.A. degree from the Kansas City Art Institute, in Kansas City, Missouri, and an M.F.A. degree from Indiana University–Bloomington.

Born in Miami, Florida, and raised in Delaware, **Paul Andrew Wandless** works and lives in the Philadelphia, Pennsylvania, area. He holds an M.F.A. degree from Arizona State University, an M.A. degree from Minnesota State University–Mankato, and a B.F.A. degree from University of Delaware. He is on the board of directors for The Clay Studio in Philadelphia and served on the board of directors for the National Council on Education for the Ceramic Arts

(NCECA) from 2001 through 2003. He is currently a special appointee to the NCECA board for special projects. In 2002 he received the Distinguished Young Alumni Award from Minnesota State University–Mankato. Along with exhibiting his works nationally in galleries, universities, and museums, Paul gives lectures and workshops regarding his work and techniques. Some of his

clay works, oil paintings, and prints are held in private collections. He has taught as a visiting assistant professor since 1999 at various universities, including Herron School of Art–Indiana University, Lincoln University, Rowan University, and University of Delaware.

GALLERY CONTRIBUTORS

Ruth E. Allan
Wenatchee, Washington
Pages 58, 104, 111, 119 (bottom)

Wally Asselberghs
Schoten, Belgium Page 16

Tom Bartel
Bowling Green, Kentucky Page 95

No'a Ben Shalom
Pardes-Hanna, Israel Page 108

Sharif Bey
State College, Pennsylvania Page 107

Jennie Bireline
Raleigh, North Carolina Page 38

Ron Boling
New Braunfels, Texas Pages 12, 21

Steven Branfman
Newton, Massachusetts Page 107

Reg Brown
Springfield, Virginia Pages 26, 92

Richard Burkett
San Diego, California Page 115

Stephen Carter
Colchester, Vermont Page 61

Jimmy Clark
Philadelphia, Pennsylvania Page 103

Cindy Couling
Sunnyvale, California Page 110

Patrick Crabb
Tustin, California Pages 18, 99

Judith Day
Steamboat Springs, Colorado Page 67

Nicole Dezelon
Pittsburgh, Pennsylvania Page 44

Bacia Edelman
Madison, Wisconsin Page 39

Don Ellis
Cloudcroft, New Mexico
Pages 102, 105, 111

Nancy Farrell
Guelph, Ontario, Canada Page 108

Piero Fenci
Nacogdoches, Texas Pages 24, 97

Gerard Ferrari
La Crescent, Minnesota Page 94

Linda Ganstrom
Hays, Kansas Pages 14, 92, 95, 98

Sheldon Ganstrom
Hays, Kansas Page 98

Janet Glass
Arlington, Texas Page 96

Juan Granados
Lubbock, Texas Pages 94, 114

Gary Greenberg
Brookville, Pennsylvania Page 106

Melissa Greene
Deer Isle, Maine Page 103

Terry Hagiwara
Houston, Texas Pages 91, 115

Judy Harper
Seattle, Washington Pages 99, 112, 114

Karen Hembree
Odessa, Texas Page 38

Richard Hirsch
Churchville, New York Pages 31, 33

Bryan Hiveley
Miami, Florida Page 101

Shellie Hoffer
Seattle, Washington Pages 103, 112

Katie Holland
Lafayette, Indiana Page 64

David Jones
Warwickshire, England Page 112

David Joy
Philadelphia, Pennsylvania Page 113

Linda Keleigh
Neptune, New Jersey Pages 76, 80, 83

Eduardo Lazo
Belmont, California Page 109

Jan Lee
Lake Toxaway, North Carolina
Pages 90, 102, 119 (top)

Biz Littell
Steamboat Springs, Colorado
Pages 48, 105

Lisa Maher
La Jolla, California Page 91

Paul McCoy
Waco, Texas Page 100

Hilda Merom
Kfar, Veradim, Israel Page 102

Virginia Mitford-Taylor
Westminster, California Pages 104, 114

Cara Moczygemba
Indianapolis, Indiana Page 104

Rafael Molino-Rodriguez
Grand Prairie, Texas Page 54

Judith Motzkin
Cambridge, Massachusetts
Pages 104, 106

Magdalene Odundo
Santa Barbara, California Pages 107, 115

Winnie Owens-Hart
Gainesville, Virginia Page 108

Jane Perryman
Hundon, Suffolk, England Pages 96. 101

Martha Puckett
Louisville, Kentucky Page 72

Charles Riggs
Carthage, North Carolina Page 99

Linda Riggs
Carthage, North Carolina Page 99

Marcia Selsor
Billings, Montana Page 93

Rolando Shaw
Commerce, Texas Page 107

Avner Singer
Pardes-Hanna, Israel Page 108

Malcolm Smith
Bloomington, Indiana Page 100

Pat Sowell
Laguna Park, Texas Pages 91, 92, 108

Maria Spies
Woodinville, Washington Page 100

Marianne Tebbens
Radnor, Pennsylvania Page 96

Beth Thomas
Galveston, Texas Page 93

Rebecca Urlacher
Eugene, Oregon Page 68

Von Venhuizen
Lubbock, Texas Pages 17, 97

Sumi Von Dassow
Golden, Colorado Pages 73, 75, 111, 113

Matt Wilt
Edwardsville, Illinois Page 90

Susan Worley
Mountain View, California Page 109

INDEX